DEMOCRATIC REPUBLIC OF
THE CONGO

Jay Heale

MARSHALL CAVENDISH
New York • London • Sydney

Reference edition published 1999 by
Marshall Cavendish Corporation
99 White Plains Road
Tarrytown
New York 10591

© Times Editions Pte Ltd 1999

Originated and designed by
Times Books International, an imprint of
Times Editions Pte Ltd

Printed in Malaysia

Library of Congress Cataloging-in-Publication Data:

Heale, Jay.
    Democratic Republic of the Congo / Jay
    Heale.
      p. cm.—(Cultures of the World)
    Includes bibliographical references and index.
    Summary: Describes the geography, history, government,
economy, people, lifestyle, religion, languages, arts, leisure,
festivals, and food of the third largest country in Africa, a
former colony of Belgium.
    ISBN 0-7614-0874-6 (library binding)
    1. Congo (Democratic Republic)—Juvenile literature.
[1. Congo (Democratic Republic)] I. Title. II. Series.
DT644.H43   1999
967.51—dc21   98–28538
             CIP
             AC

INTRODUCTION

THE DEMOCRATIC REPUBLIC OF THE CONGO (or Zaïre as it was then named) was in the headlines every day in the early months of 1997, but the news was always about armed struggles and political figures. The country and its people seemed of little interest to the outside world.

Throughout its history, little has been known of this huge country. It holds the greatest river, the largest rainforests, the biggest city, and the richest mineral reserves of Central Africa. There is amazing wildlife and scenery, vibrant music, an enormous network of inland waterways, and unfortunately, some of the worst roads in the world. It also contains simple-living, generous people who have been robbed by their rulers and governments of almost every possibility of economic development.

Through a civil war that was more like a huge sigh of relief, Zaïre rid itself of a corrupt dictator. At the time this book was written, the newly-named Democratic Republic of the Congo had a new government and new hopes.

CONTENTS

A young refugee on the road clutches her simple belongings. The refugees from the Great Lakes are a problem the new government must resolve in order to gain international respectability.

CONTENTS

A tribal mask. The Democratic Republic of the Congo is vibrantly alive with its rich traditions and tribal customs.

GEOGRAPHY

THERE WAS ONCE A TIME when all of Africa was green. Then a shift in global climate caused by the growth of the Arctic icecap produced a drying effect on the continent, and deserts such as the Sahara and the Namib were created. Yet all through those ancient times the jungles of the Congo River basin remained. They may be the most ancient part of Africa.

If you point at the center of a map of the continent of Africa, you will discover Kisangani, the third largest city of the Democratic Republic of the Congo (or Zaïre, as it was known from 1971 to 1997). The country borders nine other countries; its size of 905,567 square miles (2.35 million square km) makes it the third largest country in Africa (after Sudan and Algeria), about a quarter of the size of the United States and 77 times as large as Belgium, the country that first colonized the area.

The country is thinly populated, with half occupied by only three people per square mile. One-tenth of the country is virtually uninhabited.

Left: **Estimates are that if the Congo River were fully harnessed, it could generate 13% of the world's electricity needs.**

Opposite: **In the Nyiragongo Volcanic Park, natural flora abound. Unfortunately, the country's national parks are plagued with poachers who hunt for food as well as for ivory or hides.**

The Congo River, with all its linked tributaries, has a total of some 8,100 miles (13,033 km) of navigable inland waterways. They are used by craft from riverboats and cargo steamers to luxury motor yachts and dugout canoes.

THE SHAPE OF THE LAND

The eastern border of the Democratic Republic of the Congo is clearly defined by the lakes of the Rift Valley, an ancient geological fault in eastern Africa. In the west, a thin strip of land gives the country a short sea coast only 25 miles long (40 km) where the Congo River reaches the Atlantic Ocean. Kinshasa, the capital, is some 320 miles (515 km) inland, on the southern bank of the Congo. Brazzaville, capital of the Republic of the Congo, is opposite, on the northern bank.

The center of this huge country consists of two major river basins of the Congo (also called the Zaïre River) and its many tributaries. Inbetween and around are high plateaus (approximately 1,700 feet or 520 m above sea level), a mixture of thick forest and rolling, sunbaked plains with mountain ranges in the east and a thin wedge of coastal plain in the west.

Forest flowers in the Kahuzi-Biéga National Park.

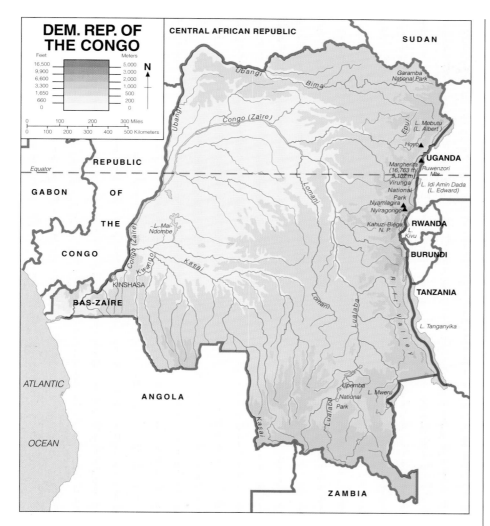

DEM. REP. OF THE CONGO

CENTRAL AFRICAN REPUBLIC

SUDAN

Ubangi

Bima

Garamba
National Park

Congo (Zaïre)

Epulu

L. Mobutu
(L. Albert)

Hoyo

UGANDA

Margherita
(16,763 ft/
5,102 m)

Ruwenzori
Mts.

REPUBLIC

Equator

Virunga
National
Park

L. Idi Amin Dada
(L. Edward)

GABON

OF

Nyamlagira
Nyiragongo

THE

Lomami

Kahuzi-Biéga
N. P.

RWANDA

L.
Kivu

L.-Mai-
Ndombe

CONGO

BURUNDI

Congo (Zaïre)

Kasai

Kwango

KINSHASA

Lomami

TANZANIA

BAS-ZAÏRE

Lualaba

L. Tanganyika

R I F T   V a l l e y

ATLANTIC

ANGOLA

Upemba
National
Park

L. Mweru

Lualaba

OCEAN

Kasai

ZAMBIA

The vast Congo basin contains about 80% of the tropical rainforest in Africa. For anyone trying to cross the Democratic Republic of the Congo by road, the main impression is of towering, steamy forests threaded by deeply-rutted "roads" impossible to use without a sturdy four-wheel-drive vehicle. It is an exotic world colored with tropical birds, red-earth termite mounds, and clouds of multicolored butterflies.

RAINFALL

The average annual rainfall is around 60 inches (152 cm) in the north and about 50 inches (127 cm) in the south. The regions north of the equator have a more defined dry season from December to February and a rainy season from April to October. Areas south of the equator are dry from April to October and wet from November to March but are just as hot and humid. Global warming is likely to make the climate more humid in the future, with a high risk of flooding at the estuary of the Congo River.

An aerial view of Kinshasa in 1976 does not show the poverty that exists in many areas of the city.

KINSHASA

The capital city is situated at the point where river traffic heading from the coast must stop because of the rapids downstream. Passengers disembark and cargo is offloaded; all continue by rail toward the Atlantic coast and the port of Matadi. Kinshasa (once called Léopoldville) is a huge city of 4.5 million people, most of whom are desperately poor and constantly in search of employment. A few rich government officials or foreign traders live in heavily guarded mansions or in hotels such as the Intercontinental. Two of the largest supermarkets were destroyed during the riots in 1991. Now all shops have difficulty obtaining stock as there is no money for buying or spending. As with all colonial towns, separate sections for Europeans and Africans were originally built; there is still a clear distinction. The affluent suburb of Gombe ("GOMB") near the river has its paved streets and electricity; elsewhere are endless areas of small, square houses built of concrete blocks, roofed with rusting corrugated iron and backed with lean-to shanties and dusty yards.

CLIMATE

In such an enormous country, it is hardly surprising to find variations in climate. The central forest basin has an equatorial climate—the equator runs south of Kisangani; its location is marked by a stone pillar beside the road. In this area, it is very hot, rarely below 75°F (24° C), with swelteringly high humidity and rain throughout the year. In the highlands to the east it is cooler, an average of 65°F (18° C), because of the height. The Atlantic coast is affected by the cold Benguela Current, which reduces the heat and humidity from time to time. Inland from the coast in Kinshasa, the high humidity can make visitors feel dizzy and sick. There is an almost permanent heat haze over the city, so that the sun glares from a hazy, white-hot sky. Yet in the high plateau country in the east and south, the prevailing winds that blow from the southeast much of the year produce lower temperatures: sometimes near freezing at night.

The richly fertile soil (especially that in the eastern highlands which is volcanic in origin) could produce enough food to feed half of Africa, but the country is so poor that at present its people do not produce enough to feed themselves.

A banana plantation and village huts nestle in tranquil slumber in the heat.

CONGO RIVER

"Going up that river was like traveling back to the earliest beginning of the world, when vegetation rioted on the earth and the big trees were kings."

—Joseph Conrad, in his novel Heart of Darkness

The word *zaïre* is a traditional African name for big rivers, so this great African river is called either the Zaïre or the Congo after the old kingdom of Kongo that existed before European settlement. The second longest river in Africa after the Nile, the Congo rises in the mountains near the western Rift Valley system and curves north, west, and then southwest past Kinshasa and Brazzaville to reach the Atlantic Ocean at Moanda. It crosses the equator twice, flowing through both northern and southern hemisphere climatic zones; thus there is always a rainy season somewhere in its huge basin. The potential for hydroelectric power is enormous; its water volume is second only to that of the Amazon. The main river channel is about 2,720 miles long (4,377 km) and up to 10 miles (16 km) wide.

There are more than 4,000 islands in the river, many inhabited by fishermen. The main tributaries are the Ubangi in the north, which forms the border with the Republic of the Congo, and the Kasai in the south, which rises in Angola and flows northward to join the Congo upstream from Kinshasa. The tributaries drain an area of over 1.5 million square miles (3.9 million square km).

The Congo delta is an area of lush green islands and endless reed marshes. The river is navigable for 84 miles (135 km) from its estuary to the port of Matadi. The next stretch of 280 miles (450 km) is full of rapids and waterfalls. Then the waterway is clear again from Kinshasa to Kisangani, a distance of over a thousand miles (1,610 km).

"It was peculiar what a feeling of hatred the river inspires one with. One hates it as if it were a living thing—it is so treacherous and crafty, so overpowering and relentless in its force and overwhelming strength ... The Congo river god is an evil one, I am persuaded."

—from the diary of A.J. Mounteney Jephson, who accompanied Stanley on his relief mission to find Livingstone in 1887

SIR HENRY MORTON STANLEY

A Welsh boy, John Rowlands, sailed as a cabin boy to New Orleans where he was adopted by a cotton broker, Henry Morton Stanley, and took his name. He served in the Confederate Army in the American Civil War. Later, as a special correspondent for the *New York Herald*, he accompanied a British military expedition to Ethiopia. The *Herald* sent Stanley to find David Livingstone, who had set off to discover the source of the Nile and had apparently disappeared. Crossing Africa from Zanzibar, Stanley found Livingstone on November 10, 1871, with the famous words, "Dr. Livingstone, I presume?" In later expeditions, Stanley sailed round Lake Victoria and Lake Tanganyika, before navigating much of the Lualaba and Congo rivers. In the employ of King Léopold II of Belgium, he built a road from what is now Kinshasa to Kisangani. In later life he became a British subject once again, served as a member of Parliament, and was knighted.

Opposite: **Ferries are a vital link in a region where roads are few and often impassable.**

MINING DISTRICT

Situated on a 4,000-foot (1,219 m) high plateau in the far southeast corner of the country, away from the steamy jungle heat, Lubumbashi is an area of dry climate and bush-covered plains. Once there were a quarter million Belgians in Lubumbashi; now there are probably less than 10,000.

The mineral-rich region of Shaba in the southeast was known as Katanga until 1972. Its industrial center is at Lubumbashi, and the entire area is rich with deposits of copper, cobalt, uranium, cadmium, tin, and zinc, as well as gold and silver. The expense involved in setting up mines and processing plants and the difficulty in transporting the processed minerals for export prevent Shaba from fully exploiting this underground wealth. The rail link with Kinshasa, some one thousand miles away through the jungle, is in such a bad state of repair that it is hardly usable. Many of the mining plants have been looted and all but destroyed.

Built by the copper-hungry Belgians and originally named Elisabethville after their queen, Lubumbashi is a pretty town with wide streets and old-fashioned buildings. During the copper-boom days, Lubumbashi was one of Zaïre's centers of wealth; it is still the country's second largest city.

Miners at the Kolwezi mine in Katanga (now Shaba) stand well back as a giant excavator goes into action, dwarfing the conventional bulldozer beside it.

Mbuji-Mayi, the diamond-mining center, is located about halfway between Kinshasa and Lubumbashi on a tributary of the Kasai River. One of the country's largest urban areas has grown around the town. Here diamonds are mined legally, mostly for industrial use, and illegally by families who dig and sift the red soil in any unguarded valley. To cut down diamond smuggling, those not employed by the mines are supposed to have an official permit, but this system frequently encourages corruption.

In the mining areas there are slag heaps, burnt earth, power pylons, and shacks made of old tin or sunbaked, earthen bricks. The nearest trees are farther away each month, as women harvest them for firewood. In the summer, there are swarms of moisture bees, which are attracted by perspiration, and mosquitoes. Malaria is a problem.

Tropical grasslands are brightened up with red-earth anthills, tawny grass, the occasional lush green palm tree, and pink bougainvillea. It is a mixture of dense rainforest with papaya and mango trees and cleared areas for habitation with parched, overused soil that offers little but subsistence living.

Parts of the Ituri forest, where the Pygmies live, show signs of degradation.

NORTHERN FORESTS

Much of the east and northeast of the country is covered with equatorial forest so thick and inhospitable to humans that it is virtually impenetrable. Although the country's untapped mineral riches are fairly well recognized, few people appreciate the riches contained in these enormous forests.

The timber includes mahogany, ebony, limba, and sapele, as well as raffia and sisal, which grow in the cleared areas. There are countless plants used by traditional healers that are gradually being recognized by modern medicine. There are rubber and palm trees and plants that grow wild including edible mushrooms, fruit trees like avocado and banana, and roots.

A few large-scale logging operations—mostly foreign-owned—are starting to harvest the forests. The cleared areas attract settlers whose land clearing causes erosion, though this is not yet a major problem.

In the Ituri forest in the northeast live the elusive Pygmy people; they slip easily through the tangled jungle growth. The Garamba National Park, on the border with Sudan, is the last sanctuary of the northern white rhino. At one time, visitors could view the wildlife while riding on elephants.

GBADOLITE

In the northwest, near the border with the Central African Republic, there was once an unknown village in the middle of the jungle. But because it was the birthplace of Mobutu Sese Seko, Gbadolite has been expanded far beyond its needs or importance. At the height of Mobutu's power, this "Versailles in the jungle" had the best water, electricity supply, hospital, and shopping facilities in the country. They say Mobutu flew an airplane across the Atlantic 32 times (at the country's expense) to Venezuela, in order to pick up 5,000 long-haired sheep for his Gbadolite "ranch." Visitors who arrive at the "international airport" drive along a divided highway into a town with an extravagant gold and marble palace and a huge conference center—both now deserted.

Kisangani, a sweaty place surrounded by encircling bush, is the third most important city in the Democratic Republic of the Congo. It was used as the base for the Zaïrean army's operations against Laurent Kabila's rebel forces. As a result, it has suffered from army looting on several occasions and is very rundown and damaged. Known as Stanleyville in earlier days, Kisangani is a terminus at the end of a network of river-trading stations from as far as Kinshasa. It is also the junction of several railway lines. Upriver are seven major rapids; the nearest to town is Boyoma Falls, once called Stanley Falls, where fishermen catch perch in tall, cone-shaped traps. This region is mostly busy with farming and the raising of livestock.

In Kisangani, there are more bicycles than cars on the battered streets where weeds grow in potholes. Red dust covers the town in the hot season and turns to red mud during the rains.

Left: **Fishing traps made of reeds and osiers along the Congo River form an elaborate network of cone-shaped structures.**

Opposite: **A woman sells gigantic mushrooms on the outskirts of the forest.**

A roadside market, with bunches of bananas in neat rows, is the scene of busy activity.

EASTERN BORDER

The split in the African continent known as the Great Rift Valley forms the eastern border of the Democratic Republic of the Congo. In this area is a chain of great lakes. On the shores of Lake Kivu are the once picturesque towns of Bukavu and Goma, popular with visitors on their way to see the lowland gorillas in the Kahuzi-Biéga National Park or mountain gorillas in the Virunga National Park. With such tourism potential, Goma was at one time "Zaïre's window to the world." The airport was well-equipped and presentable. Once the area was overrun by Rwandan refugees in 1994 and became the starting point of resistance by Kabila's rebel army, tourism became a thing of the past. In places the forest-covered hills have turned into bare, muddy ground because of the presence of refugees. Every day thousands walk a little farther into the forest to chop firewood. The southern part of this border is formed by Lake Tanganyika, an incredibly deep, freshwater lake well-stocked with fish. The roads thread their way through plantations of coffee, tea, and banana palms.

VIRUNGA NATIONAL PARK

Virunga, on the Rwanda and Uganda borders, is one of the oldest and most spectacular national parks in Africa. It holds one of the world's largest populations of hippo (around 25,000), as well as groups of the famous mountain gorillas. The terrain is a mixture of grassy plains and marshy river-mouths at the lower levels and equatorial mountain forest and snowfields in the higher areas. With abundant rainfall, bamboo is said to grow up to three feet (about one meter) a day.

Many tourists used to combine viewing the natural life of Virunga with a visit to the neighboring volcanic park with its active volcanoes Nyiragongo (which last erupted in 1977) and Nyamlagira (which last erupted in 1938). When warfare and the refugee problem die down, Virunga National Park will surely return to tourist popularity.

Virunga National Park lies completely within the borders of the Democratic Republic of the Congo. The famous gorilla sanctuary area, a World Heritage Site, is adjacent on the east and spans the borders of the Democratic Republic of the Congo, Uganda, and Rwanda. It was from this sanctuary that Dian Fossey led a campaign to save the mountain gorillas from extinction—and where, in December 1985, she was found brutally hacked to death by still unknown assailants.

The snow-capped Ruwenzori mountains alongside Lake Mobutu are spectacular and popular with climbers. The central peak, Mt. Stanley, has two summits: Mt. Margherita at 16,763 feet (5,107 m) and Mt. Alexandra at 16,750 feet (5,103 m). Villages are often perched on terraces carved out of the hillsides.

PLANTS AND ANIMALS

With so much of the country inaccessible because of the tangled forests and the muddy dirt tracks that pretend to be roads, it is not surprising that there is a rich and varied store of vegetation and wildlife. The equatorial forests contain rubber trees, valuable hardwood timbers, and fruit trees, including bananas, coconut palms, and plantains. Tropical flowers abound; perhaps the most amazing are those on the Ruwenzori mountains. There giant heather plants grow as high as 15 feet (4.5 meters) compared to two feet high elsewhere, and blue-flowering lobelia plants shoot up 10 feet (3 meters) above a vivid green carpet of moss.

The many rivers teem with fish and the coastal waters boast whales and dolphins. Reptiles include pythons in the forests, cobras, and other snakes almost everywhere, and the expected chameleons and lizards.

This beautiful viper is hard to detect among the brown leaves on the forest floor.

GORILLAS

Africa's mountain gorillas are the most famous of all the larger wildlife. One of their last remaining sanctuaries is in the Virunga mountains. According to a count taken in 1989, about 32 families remain (with around 10 individuals in each family) of which 20 were in the Democratic Republic of the Congo. Although their body hair and skin are black, the older males develop grey hair on their back and have been nicknamed "silverbacks." A silverback leads a family group that includes one or two younger males, several females, and their young. Perhaps as few as 10,000 of these magnificent creatures survive, all in the forests of Central Africa.

Gorillas are strictly vegetarian. They feed mostly on bamboo shoots but also eat berries, nettles, and wild celery. Feeding times are early morning and late afternoon, and they can sleep as much as 12 hours through the evening and night. The gorillas seen in zoos are almost all the smaller, lowland gorillas, which also live in the Democratic Republic of the Congo. Human contact has brought an extra threat to their already endangered existence: they are catching human diseases such as measles. When thousands of refugees fled through the Virunga reserve into Zaïre, the great apes were forced into colder, higher areas where they now run the risk of catching pneumonia. Some have already died in game traps set to catch other animals for food. These great apes are now trapped inside a shrinking forest that remains a war zone.

Only about 30 northern white rhino still exist outside of zoos, and these few are in the Garamba National Park. To guard them against poachers, rangers have implanted tiny radio transmitters in their horns.

THE ECOSYSTEM

Inside the rainforests there are several layers of life, each with its own ecology. On the forest floor where hardly any sunlight filters through, it is hot, dark, and damp. This level shelters browsing animals, lichen, and fungi, as well as fish and reptiles in the pools. Immediately above ground level is the understory where many varieties of monkeys swing through the twisting liana creepers. Perhaps 100 feet (30 meters) above ground is a thick canopy of leaves and branches, home to the many varieties of birds. Towering above them are the shoots of the emergents, the new growth reaching toward the sun.

Although these huge trees and the rich store of plant and animal life may look dense and strong, they are actually fragile. Because each plant and animal is interdependent, the system is quickly damaged by any disturbance. Uncontrolled logging operations do more than just cut down trees: they destroy habitat.

The forested areas are home to elephants, chimpanzees, gorillas, several species of monkeys and baboons, and rare creatures such as the okapi and the giant wild boar. In the grasslands, lions and leopards hunt buffalo and antelopes, followed by the scavengers: jackals, hyenas, and vultures. The rivers still abound with crocodiles and hippos; both are dangerous to human beings who leave them well alone.

Birds include brightly colored parrots, quaint pelicans, many species of sunbirds, and birds raised or hunted for food: pigeons, ducks, geese, and everywhere scrawny chickens. Eagles and hornbills fly over the grasslands. There are insects everywhere. Mosquitoes carry malaria; tsetse flies cause sleeping sickness; midges infest any moist area.

The **Congo breadfruit** is one of the many fruit-bearing trees that are cultivated.

BONOBO

Most people have heard of two of the African apes, the gorilla (*Gorilla gorilla*) and the chimpanzee (*Pan troglodytes*). Few know of the pygmy chimpanzee or bonobo (*Pan paniscus*) that lives almost exclusively in the rainforests of the south bank of the Congo River. They are the closest living relatives of humans. The bonobo is known to be more intelligent than the other apes and visually is nearer to human beings in appearance.

While the larger chimpanzee roams a distinct territory in groups of about 40, the bonobos form smaller and more permanent family groups that forage on their own. Because their food (mostly fruit) is in good supply, there is little competition among the groups, and the bonobos have a more cohesive society with considerably less aggression displayed. They use simple tools such as stones and wood as hammers to break open nuts, and occasionally they hunt and eat meat. Though all trade in wild African apes has been banned on the grounds that they are an endangered species, no such protection order exists for the African rainforests in which they live. If these continue to be cut and cleared, gorillas, chimpanzees, and bonobos will be faced with extinction.

HISTORY

THE DIFFICULTIES OF TRAVELING through dense equatorial jungle resulted in the Congo River basin remaining unexplored long after other African countries became better known. European explorers preferred to sail around the continent rather than hack their way into the interior. No serious interest was taken in this huge river basin until about 100 years ago.

THE KONGO KINGDOM

Legends tell of a great and glorious Congolese empire ruled by the Lunda emperor Mwata Yamvo. Those who claim descent from the Lunda today consider themselves of noble ancestry. During the period referred to by European historians as the Middle Ages, the greatest of the Central African kingdoms were the Kongo, which ruled over the lower river basin (today, western Democratic Republic of the Congo and northeastern Angola), and the kingdom of the copper-working Luba people in the grasslands of Katanga (Shaba). They collected tribute in the form of produce, cloth, or slaves.

Above: **A traditional chief wears his tribal cap at a meeting of tribal leaders.**

Opposite: **Gaily dressed Congolese women dance and wave the flag of Zaïre to celebrate Independence Day.**

FIRST EUROPEAN EXPLORERS

In 1482 the Portuguese navigator Diego Cão explored the estuary of the Congo River and named it Rio de Padrão. He made contact with the Kongo kingdom in order to include it in Portugal's widening empire. Initially, the intent was to encourage trade and introduce missionaries. The king (*mani-kongo)* accepted the Portuguese warmly, converted to Christianity, and even agreed to send his son to school in Lisbon. But an increasing demand for slaves began to dominate the relationship with Portugal.

Congolese men work with chisels to remove the bust of Henry Stanley from its plinth in Stanleyville during early independence.

When the *mani-kongo* had insufficient numbers of captured enemies or local criminals for slaves, the Portuguese sent raiding parties inland using the Atlantic island of São Tomé as their base. Finding their kingdom shattered, the Kongo people retaliated. The Portuguese moved their base south to Luanda in Angola, sent troops against the Kongo and, as would happen too often in African history, European firepower crushed all opposition.

During the 17th and 18th centuries, the growing slave trade weakened this Central African region drastically. However, the Luba people and, farther south, the Lunda people became rich on iron and copper-working. Other small kingdoms grew up in the east, near the Rift Valley lakes, and added local trade goods in addition to slaves. In return, the Zanzibari slave raiders brought with them luxuries like candles, matches, and the concept of furniture such as beds and coffee tables. So, despite the depopulating effect of the slave trade, the Central African kingdoms did grow. In 1906, a German explorer, Leo Frobenius, was surprised to find towns with impressively decorated houses, avenues lined with palm trees, and people dressed in velvet and silk with well-wrought metal weapons.

In 1871 the journalist Henry Stanley achieved fame by finding Dr. David Livingstone who was thought to be "lost" in the middle of Africa. Three years later, Stanley returned as an explorer and was the first European to trace the main course of the Congo River. Early explorers had guessed that the source of the Congo was the same lake that fed the Nile. But the first explorer to chart the main stream was Henry Stanley, in 1876. He traveled downstream for over 1,600 miles (2,575 km), losing many of his men to sickness and starvation, hostile inhabitants, and wild animals, but he showed that above the rapids of the lower Congo was a vast system of navigable inland waterways. Once people realized the river was navigable, it became a main route into Central Africa. But it was never an easy way to travel.

At this time European nations were looking for a foothold in Africa. King Léopold II of Belgium hired Stanley to create inland communications for what he now claimed as his kingdom. Roads and railways could bypass the rapids and waterfalls on the river system. The scramble for African territories began.

The French tried to prevent Belgian expansion in 1880 by sending Simon de Brazza to claim the neighboring territory north of the Congo. This became Congo-Brazzaville and is now the Republic of the Congo. Today, the two capital cities, Kinshasa and Brazzaville, are separated only by the river. All embassies have their own private boats, and when hostilities allow, diplomats spend much of their time on the river.

Mounteney Jephson, who accompanied Stanley in 1887, described the Congo as "a dark, evil-looking river, all broken water and whirlpools, with its shores of black, grim-looking rocks, with heavy jungle covering the hills beyond." The rocks are black because they are of volcanic origin. Thus the soil is highly fertile, which encourages dense, impenetrable jungle growth.

SLAVERY

It is estimated that in the 16th century alone some 60,000 slaves were shipped out of the Kongo kingdom. The de-peopling of Africa to provide for the slave markets of Europe and America continued for 500 years. As Africa became regarded as a source of slaves, Africans became devalued as people. Their culture and history were increasingly dismissed as unimportant. Their European overlords felt that they were bringing "civilization" to Africa. African cultures were ignored and crushed. It is hardly surprising that after independence in 1960, one of the first things Zaïreans in Kinshasa did was to pull down the statue of King Léopold II.

BELGIAN COLONIALISM

During the Berlin Conference of 1884–85, the Congo Free State was awarded to King Léopold II of Belgium. There was nothing "free" about its ownership; Léopold treated the country as his own private property.

King Léopold II of Belgium wanted the profits from the sale of rubber, which was already being used to waterproof boots and raincoats.

Africans were considered uncivilized and had no legal right to own land. They were duty-bound to hand over the produce of the land they worked to the owners. Every village was ordered to provide four people a year to work as full-time slaves for the Congo Free State. These unpaid workers were sent out into the jungle to bring back rubber latex, while their wives and children were held as hostages. Some had a hand cut off as punishment for not achieving the quota imposed. Gang bosses actually produced baskets of smoked human hands to prove that they were doing their job properly.

Land and mineral rights were granted to companies that would build roads and railways. Men were chained together to provide the labor required. Léopold robbed the wealth of the land and put it in his own bank account. He used much of the money to build ostentatious palaces and public buildings in Belgium, and some to bribe journalists not to report on the situation.

Missionaries who were trying to bring a little peace and education to the Congolese were horrified. Reports of the atrocities so embarrassed the Belgian government that they persuaded their king to hand over the governing of the country, which became the Belgian Congo in 1908.

For the next 50 years, the Congolese experienced a more relaxed Belgian rule, which continued to reap material profits from the country but was not so brutal. The colonial attitude toward Africans was well expressed by Dr. Albert Schweitzer, who made it clear, in 1921, "I am your brother, it is true, but your elder brother."

INDEPENDENCE

In 1958 France allowed Congo-Brazzaville to become self-governing. In the Belgian Congo, political parties had only been allowed for three years. Rioting in Léopoldville, the capital, forced Belgium to send troops in increasing numbers but without much effect. So, reluctantly, independence was granted in 1960—without sufficient planning or infrastructure. The hurriedly arranged election was won by the party headed by Patrice Lumumba, who became prime minister. After considerable disagreement, Joseph Kasavubu, Lumumba's closest rival, was named president.

Six days later, during general unrest caused by political parties unrepresented in the new power structure, the army mutinied over a pay dispute. Five days after that, the province of Katanga (now called Shaba) seceded. It was soon joined by neighboring Kasai.

In a dramatic moment in the history of the country, the Belgian premier, Gaston Eyskens, signed away Belgium's ownership of Belgian Congo to the new Congolese prime minister, Patrice Lumumba.

This statue showing Africans freeing themselves from their bonds was created for the Congo's Independence Day by Congolese students of the Art School at the Catholic mission in Kinshasa.

CIVIL WAR

The new government could not accept Katanga's independence since Katanga controlled the hugely profitable copper industry. Katanga province appealed to Belgium for military aid, and civil war broke out. Lumumba asked for help from the United Nations and peacekeeping forces were sent. But Lumumba was killed after General Joseph Mobutu launched a coup in support of Kasavubu.

MOBUTU'S RULE

After the UN troops left, the governing coalition led by Moise Tshombe was defeated by Kasavubu, who once again installed himself as president, supported by Mobutu. In 1965 Mobutu launched a second coup, with the support of the US Central Intelligence Agency (CIA), and made himself head of state. This was in the period of the Cold War between the United States and the Soviet Union and their allies. By declaring that he was an enemy of communism, Mobutu ensured that the United States (through the CIA) was firmly on his side.

In due course Mobutu started a program of Africanization. He changed his own name, ordered his people to replace Christian names with African ones, and altered any place names that he considered a link with colonialism. The country itself was renamed Zaïre in 1971.

As long as copper prices remained high, the economy of Zaïre was stable. Mobutu gave more power to those local chiefs he counted as his friends, and began a systematic milking of the country's wealth.

In 1977, Katangan rebels living in Angola invaded Shaba province, captured the mining town of Kolwezi, and massacred European workers and missionaries. Mobutu's army was clearly reluctant to fight, so the area was recaptured with the aid of Moroccan and Belgian mercenaries, with the United States providing aircraft.

When copper prices plunged in the 1970s, the country found itself badly in debt with high unemployment and increasing inflation. By the 1980s, Zaïre was bankrupt. Foreign countries kept providing support and military aid, apparently because Mobutu promised to prevent Soviet expansion in Central Africa.

Anti-Mobutu sympathizers were beaten, jailed, or eliminated. When even his foreign friends started to object to his dictatorial rule and the suppression of human rights, Mobutu allowed opposition parties to be formed only in 1990.

Mobutu indulged in reckless extravagance and neglected to pay the army. In the late 1980s, when diplomats, businessmen, and journalists were invited to a luncheon banquet in his palace in Gbadolite, French champagne was offered along with Belgian delicacies flown in that morning and served on gold plates. Mobutu's army threatened to mutiny because they had not been paid; eventually, in 1991, they started a wave of widespread looting, still remembered as the *pillage* ("pee-YAHJ"). The soldiers smashed their way into shops and the houses of Europeans. They stole anything that seemed of value: doors, kitchen sinks, tiles, light fittings, even the pipes in the walls. Men walked off with bicycles that they did not know how to ride. They took ambulances to transport the goods they had stolen.

A woman carries a sewing machine on her head during a period of looting in Kisangani in 1997.

> *"We abandon him
> as he abandoned
> us."*
>
> *—a resident of
> Kinshasa, speaking of
> Mobutu Sese Seko*

MOBUTU

The boy from the Ngbandi ethnic group who grew up in the jungle village of Gbadolite and was christened Joseph Désiré Mobutu ended his life in exile in Morocco in September 1997, one of the richest ex-presidents in the world. He had renamed his country, its main cities, its main river, and himself. His chosen new name was Mobutu Sese Seko Koko Ngbendu wa za Banga, which (according to a government authorized translation) meant "the all-powerful warrior who, because of his endurance and inflexible will to win, will go from conquest to conquest leaving fire in his wake." In African style, it was a "praise name."

Mobutu's father was a domestic cook. After attending a Catholic primary school, Mobutu won a place at the missionary high school in Coquilhatville (now Mbandaka) where he was first in his class. But he was expelled for going to Léopoldville (Kinshasa), which was strictly out-of-bounds and considered by the missionaries to be a sinful city. As part of his punishment he was also sentenced to six months in prison and then seven years in the army. He served first as a pay clerk and was then assigned to military headquarters in Léopoldville where he rose to the rank of sergeant-major. In 1956 he was allowed to leave the army. Always a keen reader, he decided to become a journalist and in due course became an editor on *Actualités Africaines* ("AK-too-AL-ee-tay AF-ree-kayn"), the first weekly paper written "for Congolese by Congolese."

During this work he met Patrice Lumumba in 1957, when the country was preparing for its first municipal election. Bitter at the constraints of colonial rule, Mobutu went to Brussels to argue successfully for the release of his friend Lumumba, who had been imprisoned by Belgian authorities in the Congo as a disruptive politician. After Lumumba's party won the 1960 election, he rewarded Mobutu with a post as colonel in the army. The arrival of United Nations forces aggravated an already confused military situation, which allowed Mobutu to build up his own private army. When a political struggle exploded in September 1960 between Lumumba and Kasavubu, Mobutu took over the government in a military coup.

REFUGEES FROM THE GREAT LAKES

To understand what happened in Zaïre in the mid-1990s, one must look to the Great Lakes region and the small countries of Rwanda and Burundi that are surrounded by Zaïre, Uganda, and Tanzania. The Banyamulenge, a tribal group related to the Tutsi people of Rwanda, moved to eastern Zaïre about 300 years ago. In 1994 there was an uprising in Rwanda and Hutu soldiers slaughtered Tutsi people who then retaliated and drove the Hutu out of Rwanda. Some 700,000 Hutus fled to refugee camps in Zaïre, occupying the Banyamulenge's territory. Claiming they were destabilizing the region, South Kivu told the 300,000-strong Banyamulenge community to leave.

A little boy holds on to his mother's skirt during the Hutu exodus from Zaïre.

ENTER KABILA

Aware that the Hutu were planning to use their lands as a launching pad for attacks on Rwanda, the Banyamulenge became rebels. They went on the offensive against both the Hutu militia and the Zaïrean army. They bombarded a Hutu refugee camp with rockets, mortars, and heavy artillery. In panic, 700,000 refugees started heading back toward Rwanda. When the foreign powers that had considered sending in troops saw that the refugees were returning to their own country, there seemed no need for international intervention. Aircraft promised by Libya did not arrive, nor did troops from Egypt. So the rebels prospered.

By November 1996 they had seized the towns of Goma and Bukavu. They were supported by Rwanda, Uganda, and Zambia. Although the rebel leader Laurent Kabila later insisted that his forces came from the many ethnic groups of Zaïre, it was in the Great Lakes that it all began.

Supporters of Kabila fly the flag of Kabila's Alliance (four opposition groups) to welcome his rebel army.

KABILA

Laurent Kabila was born on a ranch in Shaba province, one of a sub-tribe of the Luba people. He studied political philosophy at a French university and returned to the Congo to start his political career shortly after the country gained independence from Belgium in 1960. When Lumumba was killed in 1961, Kabila fled to Tanzania and from there he mounted attacks into the Congo for 10 years. He forged strong ties with President Museveni in Uganda and with Paul Kagame who led the Tutsi rebel army that took power in Rwanda in 1994.

When Kabila emerged in October 1996 as the leader of a rebel army, he seemed to represent the change that people in the Congo (then Zaïre) wanted so much. To the surprise of the world, his victorious march across the country was not the bloodbath that had been expected.

Described by a journalist as a mixture of arrogance and ignorance, Kabila is known to his supporters as *Mzee,* a respectful Kiswahili term meaning "Grand Old Man." He has been deliberately vague on his intentions, suggesting that his alliance will run a transitional government for a year before holding elections. He is backed by the rulers of Uganda, Rwanda, and Ethiopia.

For seven months, Kabila's growing army surged across the country. The only opposition came from Mobutu's own presidential guard and his foreign mercenaries. Kabila's earliest successes came in the Great Lakes region. In March 1997 his forces took the military garrison town of Kindu, a railway depot on the Congo River. Within a month, the rebels controlled Kisangani (after Mobutu's troops abandoned the city) and the diamond capital of Mbuji-Mayi halfway toward Kinshasa.

Mobutu asked South Africa's president, Nelson Mandela, to mediate, but Kabila agreed to talks without accepting any ceasefire. Meanwhile, in April, Kabila captured Lubumbashi, key to the mining industry.

In seven months, Kabila had captured nearly half the country. Mandela brought Southern and Central African leaders together in South Africa, and they all agreed that Kabila's success was inevitable. On May 17, 1997, Mobutu's senior generals told him that they could not defend Kinshasa. Mobutu agreed to resign, changed his mind, then finally left Zaïre around midnight.

A young Laurent Kabila stands outside a car carrying rebel president Gaston Soumialot, on July 27, 1964—just after Congolese Premier Tshombe threatened to suppress the communist-backed rebellion with force.

"My long years of struggle were like spreading fertilizer in a field. But now, it is time to harvest."

—Laurent Kabila

35

GOVERNMENT

AFRICANS REQUIRE A CHIEF they can look up to. He must be powerful enough to help them and to solve problems. No chief will surrender power voluntarily. If he is a rogue, he must be a highly successful rogue, skillful enough to defeat any rivals. In return for his skill and leadership, it is only natural that his people will show automatic respect and present him with gifts of money or produce. So government corruption, on a mild scale, is expected.

Of course those in authority are going to be richer than the people they govern. What is not acceptable is when a chief's people are ignored and allowed to go hungry. In the West, a leader can be voted out of office; in Africa, a chief has the right to rule until he is killed or driven out.

THE COLONIAL INHERITANCE

The Congo Free State was founded by the Belgians in 1885 and was governed first as a private kingdom for Léopold II and from 1908 to 1960 as a Belgian colony. In those days, a white man had an air of authority that was respected, even feared, by the Congolese. "A beard on the face is a sign of power," they would say. The Belgians ruled and legislated not for the good or happiness of the inhabitants but for their own profit. They enslaved many of the population, made them work for the advantage of Belgium, and took the profits home. In doing so, they set up an administrative framework of local governors and courts to hear local grievances. They also built a good network of roads and the beginning of a railroad network.

Above: **A Pende chief wears an impressive headdress, a symbol of his chieftainship.**

Opposite: **A Mayi-Mayi militia youth carries a gun and wears a wreath on his head.**

Moise Tshombe, president of Katanga (Shaba), reviews his new presidential guard in February 1961.

CONGOLESE POLITICS

As the tide of world opinion turned toward encouraging African independence, the Belgians appointed the first Congolese as members of the Governor General's Advisory Council in 1947, but gave them a limited role. These first Congolese politicians learned some political skills through their association with the trade unions.

Patrice Lumumba was one of those who started the first friendly associations for workers in the mid-1950s called *Amicales* ("AM-ee-KAHL"). Then in October 1958, he formed the *Mouvement National Congolais* (MNC), with a public declaration that "independence is not a gift to be given by Belgium, but a fundamental right of the Congolese people." When this surge of independent thought led to riots, the MNC was dissolved and its leaders imprisoned. But Belgium did agree to hold elections, which would be followed by its withdrawal from the colony.

Trying to make up for its years of inaction, the colonial administration appointed 700 Africans to senior civil service posts that had been previously reserved for Europeans. In 1959, Belgium passed a tough law against racial segregation.

Independence was declared on June 30, 1960, together with the first constitution and the establishment of six autonomous provincial governments. In the first national election the MNC won a majority and Lumumba was elected prime minister. Then the excitement was wrecked by violence as the Congolese Force République mutinied against its white officers, completing the collapse of the colonial administration.

Taking advantage of the state of turmoil, Moise Tshombe declared independence for Katanga on July 11, and southern Kasai did the same one month later. Tshombe called in Belgian troops, while Lumumba enlisted the help of UN troops.

President Kasavubu dismissed Prime Minister Lumumba, who declared the president deposed. The army tried to "neutralize" both men but soon showed itself as the ally of Kasavubu. Lumumba was held under house arrest, escaped, was recaptured, and sent to Katanga where he and two colleagues were murdered.

In 1961 UN forces ended Russian technical aid, causing considerable tension between the United States and the Soviet Union. Tshombe succumbed to UN pressure and agreed to integration for Katanga in January 1963. Then UN Secretary-General Dag Hammerskjold was killed in a plane crash while trying to bring about a ceasefire in the civil war. Into this political uncertainty came General Joseph Mobutu.

Patrice Kasavubu, the first president of independent Congo in 1960. He and Moise Tshombe came from the powerful Kongo and Lunda tribes respectively while Patrice Lumumba was from the small Batetela tribe.

Mobutu gives a press conference, wearing his characteristic leopard-skin cap.

THE POWER PLAY AROUND MOBUTU

Mobutu came to power in the 1965 coup and was elected president in 1970. Although he professed a faith in democracy, he censored the press, threatened opponents with violence, and manipulated the political situation by starting his own opposition parties in 1990 when he was under pressure from foreign governments to revive a multiparty system.

In the days before Mobutu, there were three labor unions: one Christian, one socialist, one liberal. In November 1965 all three were forced to merge into the National Union of Congolese Workers, which thus became another area controlled by the state.

Despite Mobutu's Africanization of place names, he did little to Africanize his government, which exploited the opportunity for corruption. The colonial structures stayed in place and self-interest was the norm.

MOBUTISM

One of the words coined by the international press was "Mobutism," signifying the highly African-slanted viewpoint of the Zaïrean president. Another word was "kleptocracy," to describe state-sponsored corruption.

Mobutu developed his absolute power by intimidation. Nguza Karl-I-Bond, for example, was Zaïre's foreign minister in the early 1970s, then political director of the *Mouvement Populaire de la Révolution* (the country's only legal political party). Presumably because he felt Nguza knew too much and presented some sort of threat, in 1977 Mobutu had him accused of high treason and sentenced to death. Instead, he was tortured and a year later set free. A year after that Mobutu made him prime minister. After two more years, Nguza fled to Belgium where he produced written proof of the state corruption in Zaïre and traveled on to Washington, DC, to provide the US Congress with full details of Mobutu's money-stealing techniques. Instead of forbidding him from further office, Mobutu invited Nguza to return home, and in 1986 appointed him Zaïre's ambassador to Washington. In 1988 Nguza became foreign minister once again! Not everyone was so fortunate.

Security and intelligence were essential elements of Mobutism. The president used several intelligence agencies to keep him constantly informed about anyone expressing dissent or posing any sort of threat to the system. It was dangerous to speak Mobutu's name or write it in case the secret police were too close. People cautiously referred to him as "Uncle Mo." Mobutu maintained his own Israeli-trained presidential guard of 10,000 men. One group of them became known as *les hiboux* ("layz EE-boo," the owls) since they worked mostly by night, serving as a death squad to maintain the power of the president.

No civil servant bothered to provide service unless he was bribed to do so. Government ministers required payoffs for construction projects, teachers wanted payoffs from their students, policemen halted motorists and gave them a choice between a payoff and arrest. This was "kleptocracy." Like a universal tax, though invisible, it was known and expected by all.

"If you want to steal, steal a little in a nice way. … In a word, everything is for sale, anything can be bought in our country."

—*President Mobutu Sese Seko*

POLITICAL STRUGGLES

One of Mobutu's longstanding political opponents was Etienne Tshisekedi, imprisoned in 1980 for publishing a 52-page letter condemning dictatorship. When the country's multiparty system was introduced in 1990, Tshisekedi was chosen prime minister. Mobutu dismissed him and did so on two more occasions when parliament appointed Tshisekedi as prime minister.

Another opponent was Monsengwo, the Catholic archbishop of Zaïre. In 1992 he gathered together a Grand Council of Mobutu's opponents and together they worked for four years to draft a plan for the transition to democracy.

Mobutu's final opponent was, of course, Laurent Kabila. His opposition crystallized in October 1996 with the alliance of four groups: his own Popular Revolutionary Party (PRP), the National Council of Resistance for Democracy (NCRD), the Revolutionary Movement for the Liberation of Zaïre (RMLZ) led by Masaso Minitaga Ndiaka, and the People's Democratic Alliance (PDA) led by Deo Bugera.

JUSTICE, AFRICAN STYLE

There is, officially, a supreme court in Kinshasa, as well as 11 courts of appeal, 36 courts of first instance, and 24 peace tribunals in the country. Each of the regions outside of Kinshasa has a regional commissioner and six councillors, all appointed by the president. It was ruled in 1968 that African customary law was as valid as written (Western) law and could be applied by the courts as long as it did not threaten public order. In most regional courts, a case is heard by a tribunal: a judge and two assessors.

Many Congolese prefer to appeal to traditional village decision-making, presided over by tribal elders who listen to the contending parties. The proceedings take several days; music and dancing sustain onlookers' interest. When the judgement is announced, the two opponents drink from the same cup to show there is no animosity.

"One day, when Mobutu is overthrown, they will tear down his statues, burn his pictures, curse his name and pay allegiance to a new chief."

—David Lamb, prophetically in *The Africans*, published in 1984

The Palais de la Nations in Kinshasa is a building of elegant proportions.

THE ENFORCEMENT OF LAW AND ORDER

How much was left of the military structure of the country in 1998 was anyone's guess and probably a security secret. Mobutu claimed to have his own special presidential guard (which doubled up as his personal bodyguard), three divisions of infantry, and parachute, armored, and independent infantry brigades—a total of some 25,000 men. The 1,300-strong navy included 600 marines. The air force had about 1,800 personnel, some 20 combat aircraft, and a dozen helicopters. The paramilitary police force of about 21,000 men and a 10,000-member Civil Guard remained unpaid for long periods during Mobutu's regime; many deserted to join Kabila's troops during 1996 and 1997.

When they were not paid, Mobutu's soldiers used to extort money at road-blocks. Rebel guards here strum the guitar and relax as they man a makeshift roadblock during Kabila's march into Kinshasa.

PARLIAMENTARY GOVERNMENT

According to the constitution of 1978, amended in 1980, the president is elected for seven years and appoints his own ministers. Parliament consists of a single body of 210 members who are elected for terms of five years. In Mobutu's time, the only political party permitted was the *Mouvement Populaire de la Révolution* (MPR), which was founded in 1967 and whose leader was automatically president and head of the National Executive Council and of the National Legislative Council. His nomination was by the Political Bureau of the MPR, whose 38 members were all nominated by him. All citizens acquired automatic membership in the MPR at birth and became members of the MPR Youth Movement as adults.

In early 1997, when he could see victory in sight, Laurent Kabila said, "We need, for the next 12 months, a transitional government that will organize free elections." When he was sworn in as president of the Democratic Republic of the Congo, Kabila issued a 15-point proclamation that gave him powers of legislation and the right to hire and fire government employees, as well as to ban political parties and demonstrations.

No sooner was Kabila settled in Kinshasa than civil war erupted across the river in Brazzaville. Angola remains in turmoil. Rwanda and Burundi are far from content. Within the Democratic Republic of the Congo, Shaba still wants to be a country on its own and diamond-rich Kasai has virtually been ruling itself for years. Perhaps the map of Central Africa is about to be redrawn. What is clear is that Africans are now trying to take control of their own destiny.

Rebels interrogate two men who were arrested and accused of being Mobutu's soldiers.

"We want change—we're willing to accept anyone, even the devil should he arrive, if it will bring change."

—*Willy Kashama, a resident of Kinshasa, in April 1997 (quoted in* Mail & Guardian*)*

45

ECONOMY

THE DEMOCRATIC REPUBLIC OF THE CONGO has the mineral resources and hydroelectric potential to be the richest country in Africa. Yet at present it is at the very bottom of the International Monetary Fund's (IMF) list of the poorest countries in the world.

ATTITUDE TOWARDS MONEY

The response to a lack of money in the country has been to print more, which lowers its value continually. Saving becomes pointless and the poor become poorer. People survive by cutting back to one meal a day. They buy nothing but essential goods in the stores. Worn clothes are mended again and again, old rubber tires are turned into sandals, and cardboard boxes become the walls of makeshift homes. In many places in the country money is so worthless that the villagers have gone back to a barter economy, exchanging produce for what is required.

"Mobutu stole everything from his people: wealth, trust, and hope. He bestowed upon them poverty, misery, and a crumbled future."

—*Mohamed Abdalla, in a letter to* TIME *magazine*

Left: **The men pass their time at a gas pump, a rudimentary version of today's gas stations.**

Opposite: **A young entrepreneur sells his wares in the city. The structure he carries on his head seems to be a creative piece of marketing.**

At a market corner in Kinshasa, women peddle fresh fruit and cooked food, almost dwarfed by the large signboard behind them.

THE CURRENCY

In April 1998 a presidential decree created the Congolese franc as the new currency for the country. Prior to this, the unit of currency was the zaïre (consisting of 100 makuta). In October 1993 old zaïre notes were replaced by new zaïre (NZ) notes at a starting rate of one NZ for 3 million zaïres. The orange-colored 1-million zaïre banknote used to be nicknamed the prostate, a mocking reference to Mobutu's illness.

The general feeling is that the local currency is worthless and daily transactions are increasingly being conducted in US dollars. In Shaba, the rates offered on the NZ are up to 20% higher than in Kinshasa. In the major diamond region of Kasai, people refuse to accept the NZ note as legal tender; they continue to use the old zaïre. The result is a flourishing black market of illegal foreign currency transactions at "local" prices.

THE WORKING MAN

In the Democratic Republic of the Congo, over 70% of the working population engage in some form of agriculture—mostly subsistence farming. About 13% work in industry. The need to supply enough food to keep the family alive is the greatest concern of most Congolese. A man in Kinshasa told a foreign correspondent in 1990, "At the time of the Belgians we were used to having three meals a day. During the First Republic we got used to two. With the coming of the Second, we're down to one."

Thanks to Mobutu's reign and policies, the country is now the poorest in Africa. The life expectancy is no more than about 47 years and a quarter of the adult population is unable to read or write. There are no jobs for 80% of the population. Women plant vegetables in the narrow strips of earth between traffic lanes in Kinshasa's potholed streets. Children wander around selling single cigarettes.

"Africa is the most successful producer of babies in recorded history and the world's least successful producer of food."

—*Blaine Harden, writing in* Africa: Dispatches from a Fragile Continent

In the east, two men wield a huge saw as they vertically saw a log.

AGRICULTURE AND FOOD

At independence, the Belgian Congo left an inheritance of plantation agriculture with a few African-style cattle ranches situated in the higher regions of the country that are free of tsetse-fly. For a while, the country continued producing enough to feed itself. Then, during the 1970s, many of the foreign-owned plantations and ranches were nationalized. Production dropped to a point when up to half the food supplies had to be imported from South Africa.

Now, over two-thirds of the population are engaged in agriculture, but only 3% of the land is under cultivation. The main food crops are cassava, plantains, bananas, sugarcane, corn, groundnuts, yams, and rice. The most important cash crop is oil palm, as palm oil is sold and used everywhere. Fruit grows wild, but there are attempts to tend the remaining plantations of oranges, mangoes, and pineapples. Other crops intended for export include coffee, rubber, and cocoa.

There are small numbers of goats, pigs, and sheep but hardly any serious livestock farming. Scrawny chickens form the main source of meat. A more reliable source of protein is fish. The annual fish catch is around 150,000 tons and comes almost entirely from inland waters.

MINING AND INDUSTRY

Beneath the surface of the Democratic Republic of the Congo are treasures uncountable. The country has an estimated 60% of the world's cobalt, as well as industrial-grade diamonds and reserves of petroleum, zinc, copper, manganese, silver, and gold. In the days of the Belgian Congo, there was no attempt at diversification. Copper seemed a satisfactory way of getting rich, so all efforts were put into that one mining industry.

Some improvements were gradually made: roads and railways were built and the European-style beginnings of several cities. The Inda Dam on the lower Congo was constructed to provide hydroelectric power, and there was an increasing appreciation of the mineral wealth in the ground. In the years after independence copper prices stayed high; during 1973 it doubled.

When President Mobutu launched his Africanization program, it removed a large number of skilled foreigners from important business positions. Then in April 1974, the price of copper collapsed. With it went any hope of rescuing the country's economy—all the financial eggs had been in one basket. The country's copper output plunged from 476,000 tons in 1986 to about 31,000 tons in 1994. However, copper still contributes about 38% of the country's export earnings; cobalt is next at about 12%. The most important mining area is Shaba, the Kiswahili word for copper, though local residents prefer its older name of Katanga. It was uranium from Lubumbashi that helped create the atomic bomb that destroyed Hiroshima in 1945. Reef gold is mined in Shaba and in the northeast of the country. There are also reserves of zinc, bauxite, tin, and iron that are almost untapped.

Above: **Two miners working in a gold mine are surrounded by a world of cavernous blue.**

Opposite: **A rubber tapper works to collect latex on a rubber plantation.**

MINERAL RESOURCES

Today, the state-owned company La Générale des Carrières et des Mines (known as Gécamines) controls all the cobalt and 90% of copper mining. There are huge reserves of cobalt, copper, gold, diamonds, and uranium waiting to be tapped, together with a huge hydroelectric power potential, but the infrastructure has been almost destroyed, and the will to work has dwindled away.

The central area around Mbuji-Mayi is the world's largest producer of industrial diamonds. Since private syndicates were allowed to mine, more gem diamonds have been discovered as well. However, most mine machinery has been looted or destroyed, the management has fled, and the workers have moved elsewhere or are starving.

During the 1980s, crude petroleum from the oil deposits off the Congo estuary became an important export. Such industries as remain concentrate on foodstuffs and beverages, with some production of tobacco, textiles, rubber, leather, wood products, cement, and building materials. But nearly all produce far below their capacity because of the poor transportation facilities, the lack of foreign exchange, and the inability of the population to buy what little is produced.

THE WEALTH OF SHABA

In early 1997, when Kabila's rebel forces were gradually taking over Zaïre, there was serious talk among high-level industrial businessmen of getting together to hire an army, to prevent the rebels taking over Shaba province. Their fear was that if the rebels took Shaba, with its vast fortune in cobalt, copper, gold, and diamonds, they would control the whole economy. While South African diplomats struggled to set up talks between Mobutu and Kabila, attempting to remain unaligned and neutral, South African mining interests (in competition with mining interests from the United States) were struggling equally hard to obtain or remain on friendly business terms.

RIVER TRANSPORTATION

When the Belgians left in 1960, the Belgian Congo had one of the finest road systems in Africa. Today it is impossible to drive from one end of the country to the other. Of a road network of some 90,000 miles (145,000 km) only 1,500 miles (2,400 km) of road are paved. The rest is dirt track that is steadily turning back into bush.

The few great rusting riverboats that ply between Kinshasa and Kisangani are a vital link in the country's disintegrating transportation system. They are state property and together with smaller river craft move a quarter of a million passengers and a million tons of freight each year.

There is an international airport in Kinshasa and reasonable airports at Kisangani, Lubumbashi, and Goma. However, the national airline, Air Zaïre, which is 80% state-owned, has always been short of planes.

A constant traffic of pirogues ply the Congo.

"The transport system, developed in the colonial era … has not changed significantly, except in many places where it has deteriorated greatly."

—*from* Africa Today *magazine*

Passengers wait to board
the train to Kisangani.

RAIL TRANSPORTATION

In 1990, only about 430 miles (692 km) of railway track were reported usable, and trains traveled very slowly for fear of derailment. A few stretches of railway, linking Kinshasa to Matadi in the west, and Lubumbashi to Kindu in the east, were upgraded by Sizarail, but a journey from Kinshasa to Lubumbashi by road and rail usually takes about two weeks.

SIZARAIL

A joint venture in 1995 backed by South Africa, Belgium, and Zaïre to repair and upgrade the country's railway system was called Sizarail. For a while it seemed a success story. Staff received regular salaries and rail journeys took days instead of weeks. Kabila's advancing rebel forces closed Sizarail on the grounds that those who operated it were "friends of Mobutu." This closure created a backlog of copper and cobalt that the country needed to export. Sizarail has now been rechristened Société Nationale des Chemins de Fer du Congo and has been put under state control.

THE *PILLAGE*

The two days of wanton destruction in 1991 was called the *pillage* (French for looting). People began to talk of life "before and after the *pillage*." It was caused by the utter frustration of the armed forces who had not been paid for months. In an effort to find cash to pay the troops, Mobutu doubled the bus fares. In retaliation, the public burned all the buses. The soldiers remained unpaid. Armed and angry, they went out of control. Civilians, just as frustrated by low wages, joined in. Mines were looted, stores destroyed, shops and factories looted and burned, hotels wrecked, trains vandalized. All hope of any economic recovery in Zaïre disappeared in the smoke. The result was 80% unemployment and a complete breakdown in the financial system. The notion of looting stayed in people's minds. On several occasions, throughout the country, it happened again. Houses belonging to Europeans were a favorite target. The looters took anything, convinced that if it came from a European house it must be valuable.

THE ROAD TO BANKRUPTCY

Two things combined to create the country's present economic disaster. The first was the collapse of the copper market, which resulted in the country incurring the world's highest international debt (over US$4 billion) in the 1980s. The second problem was the rampant corruption. The country's annual growth rate before independence had been 4.9%; it dropped to less than 2% during the 1970s and 1980s and averaged −8.6% in the 1990s.

The streets of Kinshasa littered with garbage after the demonstration and looting in November 1991.

FOREIGN AID

President Mobutu convinced Western countries that Zaïre was providing a strong opposition in Africa to the threat of world domination from the Soviet Union. To counter the threat of spreading communism, the United States and its allies provided over $1 billion in aid. They also thought that Zaïre was a useful base for intelligence operations in Central and Southern Africa. This foreign aid was used to support the increasing power of the state: training and equipment for the police and armed forces, as well as emergency food during droughts. An international grant of $1.8 million intended for the repair of Kinshasa's broken-down city buses was reduced to $200,000 by the time it reached the ministry of transport.

Children and young men gather around a village well, collecting water from the tap.

A BLEAK FUTURE

Mobutu is gone. In his place is Kabila. What lies in store for the Democratic Republic of the Congo?

During the rebel advance, the future was made to look understandably rosy. When his troops arrived in Kisangani, Kabila announced that there would be a 50% cut in income tax and a 50% reduction in the prices of beer, water, electricity, and fabric; in Goma he decreed that house rents should be halved.

There are high hopes for a resumption of mining profits countrywide. An increase in gold production is also planned. Kabila's promises include new roads, economic development, an end to corruption, and justice for all. But Mobutu left the country saddled with an international debt about 200 times greater than the gross domestic product, so there is no cash for structural improvements.

Congolese smugglers from Kinshasa to Brazzaville cling onto the bridge in a clandestine crossing.

Where has the wealth of the country gone? Although there is widespread condemnation of the way that the late president robbed Zaïre, Swiss banks reported finding only US$3.4 million in assets belonging to him. Finance Minister Célestin Lwangi contends that Mobutu at one time had US$8 billion stashed away in overseas banks and has demanded further investigation. Since it was impossible to get rich in the old Zaïre without playing some part in Mobutu's corrupt, bribe-ridden system, the businessmen left in Kinshasa when Kabila arrived are understandably nervous. It was reported that of every dollar coming into Zaïre through international aid, officials took 20 cents as their personal cut. The 1977 coffee crop, for example, was valued at US$400 million, but because of smuggling and under-invoicing, only US$120 million arrived in Zaïre's treasury.

CONGOLESE

WHO LIVES IN THE AFRICAN JUNGLES and how many there are can never be established accurately. Informed guesses in 1997 gave a population figure of around 47 million people. The Population Reference Bureau in Washington, DC, has estimated that by the year 2025, the Democratic Republic of the Congo will be the third most populous nation in Africa, with 107.6 million people, after Nigeria (246 million) and Ethiopia (129.7 million). Half the population is under the age of 15.

THE ETHNIC GROUPS

The Congolese do not belong to clear ethnic groups, in spite of language similarities. There are over 200 tribal groups, and not one is more than 4% of the total population. More than two-thirds of these are Bantu, the language-related black African group that now occupies most of the southern half of Africa, as well as people of Sudanese and Nilotic-speaking (early Egyptian) origin, and groups of Pygmies. A small number of European settlers, mostly of Belgian or French origin, and an increasing, unsettled number of refugees from Rwanda, Burundi, and Angola add to the diversity.

Above: **Young men in a village pose for a group photograph.**

Opposite: **A Pygmy woman, with pierced nostrils, prepares a meal for her family in the Ituri forest.**

STATISTICS

Of the estimated 47 million population, 15 million constitute the labor force; only 25% of the labor force are wage earners.

Nearly half the population (48%) are under 15 years old and only 3% are over 65 years old.

In all age groups, females exceed males.

The population growth rate in 1997 was estimated at 2.34%.

THE KASAI are probably the strongest ethnic group. Their tribal base is around Mbuji-Mayi, the main town of the industrial diamond industry, though their influence has spread. Kasai held many of the top government posts in the days of Mobutu. It was often said that "You need to speak Kasai in order to get a good job."

THE KUBA also live in the center of the country, around Kananga. Though few in number now, they were once powerful. The Kuba kingdom reached its height 300 years ago when their 93rd king, Balongongo, became a cultural hero who was said to have introduced cassava, palm oil, tobacco, raffia, and embroidery to the area.

THE KONGO once had the most powerful kingdom in Central Africa and extended their power around the lower reaches of the Congo and south into what is now Angola. Their rulers held the title "mani" and controlled their currency by using as money special shells found only in the waters fished by their ruling family. Their dialect, Kikongo ("ki-KON-go"), is the most widely spoken language in the country, especially in Kinshasa.

THE LUBA prospered notably in the 16th century after the introduction of corn and cassava from the west. They live mostly in the Shaba region, north of Lubumbashi, and work in the copper mines. Their dialect, Tshiluba ("chi-LOO-bah"), is widely spoken in the southeast, though many speak Kiswahili ("ki-swah-HEE-lee") as well. The Baluba have a reputation as artists, and Luba masks are among the most famous of Congolese/Zaïrean craftwork. Laurent Kabila, the president, belongs to the Luba group, Mulubakat, from Shaba province.

Two young men carry bags for the climbers who visit the Nyiragongo Volcano.

THE AZANDE were late arrivals in the Congo region, invading from the northeast in the 19th century. They are a Sudanese race and have their own religion based on Mani, the god of the rainbow.

THE ALUR are a Nilotic race who live on the shore of Lake Mobutu (also called Lake Albert). Their culture is dominated by traditional kings and by priests who claim to possess the art of rainmaking. Their features are slightly more European than African, with a very dark brown skin color.

THE MAKERE live near the Bima River in the northeastern forests. Makere mothers still have the custom of winding strips of cloth around the heads of their newly-born daughters so that the skull becomes elongated in what they consider a fashionable shape. Their area was prime hunting country for Arab traders, who took many women and children hostage in exchange for ivory.

Azande children at play are relaxed and happy, looking after the smaller ones in the group.

THE LUNDA were once a proud Congolese empire led by a legendary king, the Mwata Yamvo. The northern descendants of the Lunda still live in Shaba province, but many have moved to Angola and Zambia and now speak a totally different language. Some still press for Shaba (Katanga) to break away as a separate country, hoping to revive the Lunda empire.

THE CHOKWE were originally a seminomadic Bantu-speaking people near the Upper Kwango and Kasai Rivers. Many became slavers for the Portuguese and so helped to destroy many neighboring kingdoms including that of the Lunda. Known for their skill in carving sculptures of human and animal forms, the million and more Chokwe are now spread over a wide area that includes the southern Democratic Republic of the Congo as well as adjacent parts of Angola and Zambia.

A Lunda chief arrives at a meeting to discuss economic problems in 1959.

PYGMIES

A typical Pygmy is little more than four feet (1.2 meters) tall. He has brown rather than black skin, brown eyes, a snub nose, and thin lips. The older men may have a sparse, tufty beard. These small-sized warriors of the northern rainforests were most probably the earliest inhabitants of the Congo basin. Nomadic, they move around in small groups, rarely settling anywhere for long. They live by hunting and fishing, combining in groups, often using dogs. Both men and women gather food from the forests they know so well, collecting honey, nuts, and roots. Women tend their settlements and sometimes grow peanuts. The Pygmies are pacifists by nature and hardly quarrel in a group. They are also very shy and if surprised by the approach of strangers (which happens seldom, as they are acutely aware of all that lives around them), they will drop everything and rush off into the forest.

They value children as most precious possessions, as they must, for infant mortality is high. If parents die, children are passed on to another family group. In many groups there is no defined leader. All adults are called "mother" and "father" by all the children, and decisions are made by general agreement. The group lives in communal style with most possessions (apart from weapons) owned by all. They value life highly and will burst into spontaneous dancing and drumming, usually at night, around a fire.

Pygmies live mainly in the dense tangle of trees and undergrowth of the Ituri forest region. They avoid forest clearings, which are fiercely hot. Those near the Epulu River and Mount Hoyo are becoming used to contact with Europeans. They will sit by the road, waiting to be photographed or just talked to, and will then demand a tip. Their fellow Bantu Congolese, who trade with them for fish and forest medicines, regard the Pygmies as lazy. In turn, the Pygmies regard the Congolese as unfair in paying them too little in goods, not money, and even as downright cheats.

Luxury for a Pygmy man is a fill of tobacco that he smokes in a pipe about a yard long, using a piece of glowing charcoal to keep it lighted. Those who are in contact with civilization live in a transitional world. They make simple huts instead of the traditional domed, leaf-covered dwellings. They use home-made rifles for hunting. They hitch rides on timber trucks to reach fresh hunting grounds.

The urban Congolese dresses well in vibrant colors and matching headscarfs.

CHARACTERISTICS

The Congolese, like other Africans, know the importance of survival. In order to survive, you must have patience. To avoid stress, you move with the pace of the system. You wait patiently in line to see the doctor or apply for a permit. You do not get frustrated if machines do not work or if goods are not available in the shops. So long as you have something to eat and wear, a modest shelter to call home, and the surrounding love of your family, the world has treated you well. The Kiswahili speakers would say *Shauri ya Mungu* ("SHOW-ree yoh MUN-goo")—it is God's will.

Yet all this patience vanishes when a Congolese is put behind the wheel of a car. He becomes a totally different personality and sees the car as a challenge to his manhood. The route from Kinshasa airport to the city is probably the most used stretch of road in the country and a common place for car accidents.

The African tribal system stipulates that a man should look after his family first, then his clan, then his tribe. The idea of belonging to a nation is not an important concept. What matters more is power, which should be held by one individual and not be weakened by being shared.

THE EXTENDED FAMILY From its earliest days, a Congolese baby is strapped to its mother's back and goes everywhere she goes, working in the fields or carrying wood or water to the home. By the time the next baby arrives and takes its place on mother's back, the growing child has absorbed a strong physical presence of love and care. So the child grows up obedient to the parents and with the awareness that there is nothing more important than the family. Although a young child is often left on its own, there are always brothers, sisters, or a grandparent around. The same extended family system is found in the shantytowns around the big cities, but tends to fade away with the nuclear family groups in towns.

Women and their children on their way home, laden with water containers, take the opportunity to beg for money.

REFUGEES

The Democratic Republic of the Congo, which cannot produce enough food to feed its own people, is host to over a million refugees—mostly from Rwanda, but also from Angola, Burundi, and other war-torn neighboring countries. In 1994 the refugee camps near Goma held 300,000 people, twice the normal number of inhabitants in Goma. At the height of the influx, refugees were pouring into the country at a rate of 600 people per minute. Today, this refugee problem is a delicate political issue for the country as international aid is being withheld and the United Nations insists on access to information and "controversial" sites to investigate the possible genocide of Hutu refugees in some camps.

The Hutu exodus from the country was watched by millions of people worldwide.

DRESS

A length of cloth, tied under the arms for a woman or round the waist for a man, is the simplest and cheapest form of clothing in Africa. The poorer Congolese may add a skirt or a pair of trousers or a T-shirt, but in this hot land, no one needs a lot of clothing. Most families strive to have one good set of clothes for church or festive days.

The introduction of comparatively cheap clothing in the cities and markets has led to most urban folk dressing in conventional Western style. The men wear open-necked shirts with jeans or dark trousers, and sneakers or brown leather shoes. Older men wear a hat. Most women wear a headscarf. Short skirts or tight pants for women are frowned on as being suggestive.

Given the opportunity and the means, women will dress like royalty with a long flowing dress, ruffled sleeves, and a swathed headdress of the same material. Dressing well for urban women means imitating the latest Western styles.

City girls like to dress well. Here, they show off their latest in clothes and hairdo.

67

LIFESTYLE

THERE CAN BE NO NORMAL LIFESTYLE in a country torn apart by civil war. Although Laurent Kabila's forces have liberated the country from Mobutu's rule and have completed their military campaign, the struggle for control is far from over. There is still a general lack of law and order.

POVERTY AND STARVATION

The first and constant problem is a lack of money and food. Farmers do not grow more than their family needs because the income they would get is worthless. Inflation at one time was reportedly running at 4,000%. With no social security system and little employment, many people turned to robbery, corruption, or begging. Young men hitch a ride on an overland truck or river steamer to go to a big city where they become one more unemployed worker. Too ashamed to return home without having succeeded, they turn to crime.

In the slums of Kinshasa, there are huts so tiny that the occupants cannot all sleep at the same time. A family is hungry because there is no furniture left to sell. A mother can feed her baby only once every other day. When someone dies of malnutrition or disease, there is no money to pay for a funeral.

Left: **Two young mothers bring their babies to the market at Kamina, a town north of Kolwezi in Shaba province.**

Opposite: **Two Pygmy children at play. Millions of Congolese children grow up without ever seeing electric light, a telephone, a water tap, or any sort of enjoyable reading material.**

A truck gets stuck in one of the many deteriorating roads in the country.

GETTING AROUND

"The first problem is the roads," said a visitor. "There aren't any." During the rainy season, the tracks through forests or across wooded plains are so swampy or rocky that trucks have to be dug out of potholes as big as swimming-pools. The sensible traveler goes either by bicycle or on foot.

The highways of the country are the waterways. Riverboats as large as those on the Mississippi River churn their way between Kinshasa and Kisangani, though with considerably less glamor. Their timetable is erratic as they tend to wait until they have gathered enough cargo and passengers to make the trip worthwhile. In addition to people, they carry battered trucks, rusty bicycles, crates of chickens, and tethered animals. The smell of rotting fish pervades everything.

On river crossings, the use of ferries is supposed to be free, but the fare is usually enough diesel for them to operate. Dugout canoes known as pirogues are used by fishermen as the waterborne equivalent of a bicycle.

THE RIVERBOATS

There are usually three huge riverboats operating on the waterway between Kinshasa and Kisangani. Each has a giant, four-decked tug for first-class and *de luxe* travelers and crew, with four or five rusty barges attached with more primitive accommodation for second- and third-class travelers. This "floating city" departs from one terminus fully booked and loaded, then accumulates as much as double the load along the way until it arrives with as many as 3,000 people aboard. One European traveler described the riverboat as "an immense, stinking, noisy, overheated, overcrowded African market." Almost as many travel on the roofs of the barges as inside.

For those who live by the river, the riverboats offer an opportunity to trade. All along the route, wooden pirogues shoot out from the forested shore and attach themselves to the side of the riverboat. Their owners haul on board their goods and sell them, making vast profits for traders and the riverboat captain. Goods include cassava and monkeys, handwoven mats and edible maggots, dried catfish and live snapping turtles. The decks become a menagerie of Congolese wildlife: ducks, geese, chickens, goats, and pigs are normal; they may be joined by crocodiles, parrots, anteaters, bushbucks, or otters. Some animals die on the way and are cut up and added to the stock in the freezer or tipped overboard. Smalltime traders have permanently-booked second-class cabins that become shops selling clothing, soap, cosmetics, plastic buckets, and medicinal drugs, all at rip-off prices. As the pirogues drop off and are paddled home, more arrive. Business continues all day and night.

The well-known bush-taxi operating in much of Africa is available only in the larger towns. It may be an old Peugeot 504, a well-dented minibus, or a pick-up truck with wooden seats. Always, it will be crammed to capacity and the passengers will howl with mirth every time the vehicle jolts into yet another pothole and yet another head hits the roof. There is nothing like African humor! The railway system, built by the Belgians, used to be quite good. There is no longer a first-class service (despite the printed tickets) since there is likely to be no water or lighting available, and quite probably no windows or door. Traveling from one end of the country to the other can take a month, unless one takes an airplane.

Above: **This charming Congolese woman in the city lives differently from her country sisters.**

Opposite: **Village children enjoy the simple life in the countryside.**

CITY LIFE

The contrast between urban and rural life is distinctly marked. Kinshasa, with approximately 4.5 million people, boasts skyscrapers such as the Intercontinental Hotel with its luxurious shops and suites, while in the rainforests Pygmies live as primitive hunter-gatherers did thousands of years ago. In Kinshasa policemen wearing white gloves used to stand directing traffic under small awnings to protect them from the sun. "River people" live in rubbish-built shanties on islands and under bridges. The stench of their poverty is obvious to the rich who go boating on weekends.

When Kabila's rebel army marched into Kinshasa, there was initially very little violence. But the rebels found a city with little to be proud of. Piles of refuse lay stinking in the streets, litter blew around, few water taps or telephones worked, the buildings were grimy and damp with mold.

Yet even in that squalor and poverty, the residents continue to live and laugh. The pulse of Kinshasa is still in the vibrant African quarter with its backyard bars, street corner catering, and the live music that has given Zaïrean music an international reputation. Other cities—Lubumbashi, Kisangani, and Mbuji-Mayi—are nowhere near as large as Kinshasa. Their hotels are less luxurious, their shantytowns less populated. But they are all plagued with the same two problems: the absence of any state money to make repairs or pay officials and a steady influx of rural migrants hoping to find work, and thus food, in town.

COUNTRY LIFE

To the eyes of outsiders the rural Congolese may appear to own nothing, but this does not prevent them from offering fruit, water, or shade to welcome a visitor. Their sense of hospitality may result in a feast of roasted groundnuts, grilled corn, or elephant meat.

Most dwellings are of mud bricks or of wood with woven walls. A central meeting house or shelter called the *da* doubles as accommodation for guests. It may contain a bamboo bed or *kiri-pa* ("KEE-ree-PAH") for visitors to lie on. Smells in the air might include drying cassava, a bit like yeasty bread, or the tempting aroma of roasting meat if a hunter has returned with a kill.

The women go to the fields each day to gather what is required and restock by continual planting. They will return with cassava, which is peeled and soaked, then dried and crushed, before being pounded in a wooden mortar for cooking. This is an on-going process that may take a week or more.

Men still go hunting, armed perhaps with a shotgun or with homemade guns. Their sons practice earnestly with a bow and arrow or with catapults. There are no telephones so people shout the news down the village street.

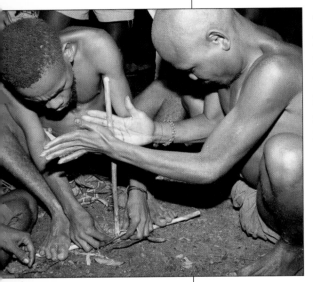

Mount Hoyo Pygmies concentrate on building a fire using sticks and friction.

EDUCATION

It is a wonder that education continues at all in a country torn by war and in which teachers have remained unpaid for long periods. However, the Congolese respect education and want their children to have its advantages in a world where jobs are ever harder to get. Primary education, from ages 6 to 12, is supposed to be compulsory. Official figures claim that between 60% and 70% of the children (more boys than girls) attend the 10,000 primary schools. Only about one million students go to one of the 4,000 secondary schools. Considering the recent lack of funding for schools and teachers' salaries, the proportion of children attending school is probably far lower. Secondary schools, where attendance is not compulsory, include schools of general education, teacher training colleges, and technical schools. There are university campuses in Kinshasa, Kisangani, and Lubumbashi.

FOREST LIFESTYLE

The Congolese have plenty of wood in their forests, but show economy and resourcefulness in making cooking fires. As with so much in Africa, it is a method that requires the least effort worked out through long years. Three logs are set in a star shape with stones in the spaces between the log-ends to rest a cooking pot on. Twigs and dry grass set the fire alight, and as the logs burn, they are pushed inward. Different woods burn differently: bamboo is hot and fast and good for boiling, jungle hardwoods burn slowly but give good coals for roasting. The skill is to know which wood will provide the temperature needed for the food being cooked.

Compared to the West, which spends an annual average of $2,400 per student, and Latin America, which spends about $280, sub-Saharan Africa spends a little over $50 per student on education. The first schools in the country were started by missionaries and these remain important.

In a rural school, pupils may sit on a bare earthen floor in a roofed shelter without windows. They are taught orally (for there are no books) from a blackboard that has to be taken down each afternoon to prevent it from being stolen.

In Kinshasa, during the months before Kabila arrived, parents refused to pay school fees. When their children were barred from class, they grumbled hopefully, "When Kabila comes, school will be free." The sad truth is that all basic social services have suffered drastically from a lack of state funding.

Young Azande boys in class.

Official figures for literacy are 68% for women, and 87% for men. Literacy here is defined as the ability to read and write in French, Lingala, Kingwana, or Tshiluba.

HEALTH

The medical facilities in the country are appalling. Equipment does not work because someone has stolen pieces of it, and often there is no electricity or water. Patients lie in hospital corridors because the wards are full, and frequently they must share a bed. At Mama Yemo General Hospital (named after Mobutu's mother) in Kinshasa, the sick must supply their own drugs, bedding, food, and syringes. Animals wander in and the state of cleanliness is highly suspect. Many health clinics have shut down because the medicines intended for their use have been intercepted and sold on the black market.

A missionary nurse feeds her patients in a children's ward.

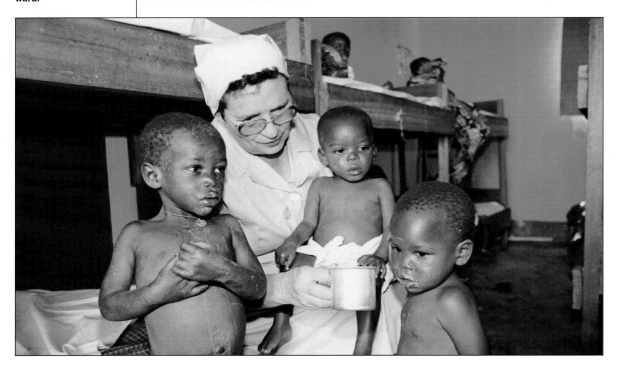

Perhaps 25% of the country's population have access to safe water, compared to 18% in the Central African Republic, 43% in Zambia, and 70% in South Africa. A lack of sustaining food and proper health care results in a mortality rate of one-third of all children before the age of 5, usually from diseases that could have been prevented. Every year malaria affects about one in five Africans and kills over a million. The moist, humid conditions of the rainforests are an ideal breeding ground for the Aedes mosquito.

Congolese mothers are aware of the risk of getting skin-worms if clothes are not ironed properly. The tumba fly lays eggs in wet clothing. The heat of ironing kills the eggs, but in damp cloth the eggs become larvae and bore into the skin where they can grow to twice the size of a grain of rice and are most painful.

Mothers give birth to many children in the hope that perhaps half of them will live. They do not understand that drinking water can affect the health of their children. Although the lakes and rivers supply plentiful fish (a useful source of protein), the lush lakeside grasses harbor the bilharzia snail, which causes blood flukes and an infection of the bladder. This is called snail fever.

Another common waterside disease is "oncho", or river blindness (*onchocerciasis*), which can be caught by swimming in a lake or a river. It causes partial or complete blindness as well as an itching under a loosened skin that is so constantly painful that some sufferers commit suicide. Food cooked with river water often causes amoebic dysentery.

Traditional healers pour herbal medicines (made with ground bark, leaves, and roots) into bottles for their clients. Their prayers, combined with the patients' faith in the process, seem to be usually beneficial.

The ebola virus, which causes severe internal hemorrhaging, first appeared in Zaïre in 1977 and returned in 1995. Fortunately, local health authorities alerted the World Health Organization swiftly, and the outbreak was restricted to just 316 cases, of whom 245 died.

AIDS (ACQUIRED IMMUNE DEFICIENCY SYNDROME)

Known by its French acronym, Sida, AIDS is devastating the population of sub-Saharan Africa. For people with an African belief in unavoidable fate, it can result in a man just sitting down and waiting to die. In 1990, the World Health Organization estimated that the number of adult AIDS cases in Africa was more than half the world total. The Democratic Republic of the Congo was listed as one of the 12 African countries with the highest incidence of AIDS.

Research has shown that some African monkeys are infected with a close relative of the AIDS virus. This, in addition to the high number of infected people in Central Africa, has given rise to the opinion that the AIDS epidemic started there. Whatever its source, the statistics are increasingly frightening. At the end of 1996, an estimated 14 million people in sub-Saharan Africa were HIV-positive or suffered from full-blown AIDS, compared to 200,000 in North Africa and the Middle East, 510,000 in Western Europe, and 13,000 in Australasia. On one-family farms, the death of a single adult male can reduce the output considerably. Africa is seeing more orphans and more empty villages.

In the Democratic Republic of the Congo, the situation was aggravated when women took to prostitution in a desperate effort to earn money. Sexual contact (the chief way in which AIDS is caught and spread) has increased. Another reason for the rapid spread of AIDS is that the Congolese, like many Africans, believe injections are more effective than pills, so they buy medication that is administered by intramuscular injection. But a shortage of syringes results in the same one being used repeatedly, without proper sterilization. The question in Central Africa seems to be not whether there will be an AIDS epidemic, but just how terrible it is going to be.

THE ROLE OF WOMEN

This is a patriarchal society. Men, especially the elders of the community, are important. Women are expected to work for their men, and they accept this role in society. It is not unusual to see an old woman staggering along a village street with a huge load of food on her head, while her husband lolls back in the doorway with an empty bottle of alcohol in his hand. Wife-beating is not uncommon.

Yet it is the women who are the backbone of every rural community. They plant and tend crops, and harvest the food. They run the markets, which are the prime economic activity of the village. Fathers acknowledge that daughters are more valuable than sons, for the females "have not forgotten how to work." Women are expected to be faithful; men can have many wives or girlfriends. Anything a woman earns is spent on her family. A man spends his money on what he chooses.

A law imposed in 1987 and known as Mobutu's Family Code gives a husband the right to claim all of his wife's property, even if they are not living together. Polygamy was legalized, at the same time relieving husbands of any responsibility for the maintenance of their women and children. As a rule, wives do not inherit from their husband and they can be divorced without settlement. Indeed, in some areas a widow is expected to pay off her dead husband's debts; this "purifies" her from the suspicion of having killed her husband. Wives today are hoping that the new government will annul this family code.

Women in the country are the pillars of family life and the economy as they struggle to manage a multitude of challenging responsibilities.

RELIGION

IN MATTERS CONCERNING RELIGION, it is essential to remember that the people of Africa have deeply rooted and ancient beliefs. Their way of thinking concerns the basic relationship between living man and the earth itself. Sunlight, water, the fruits of the trees, the rocks in the ground—all are part of the African consciousness.

A DIFFERENT STYLE OF BELIEF

It is probably true to say that all the religious groups in the Democratic Republic of the Congo believe in one god. But this god is not one to be worshiped directly. Even though he may be considered the creator and cause of all things, most Congolese people believe he is too far away and unknowable to influence their own lives. The spirits of dead ancestors form the link between humble human beings and the mightier power that other religions may call God.

Left: **A simple mud mosque in a village, a picture of tranquillity.**

Opposite: **Gaily dressed women walk past a church on their way to a celebration.**

CHRISTIANITY ARRIVES

Christianity was established in Africa well before it reached Europe. Although Christianity was first confined to the early churches in Egypt and Ethiopia, historians record that it was the Portuguese who converted the Kongo people in the area around the mouth of the Congo River, for soon after the colonizers came the missionaries. Many thought Africans unenlightened, and they regarded their duty as imposing Christian morals on a backward people, by force if necessary. Gradually that view changed to a greater respect for the rights of the indigenous people. On the whole, missionaries viewed rural village life as simple and innocent in comparison to that in the mining communities.

A church service may take place in a church or chapel, or under a canvas awning in the open air. There is much dancing and hand-clapping, and the sermon is long because it is often delivered in French with an interpreter enthusiastically translating the imposing warnings and advice into the local dialect.

THE BALANCE OF RELIGIONS

It is difficult to estimate how many people practice each religion in the country since many people are members of an established religion while staunchly refusing to give up their more traditional practices. Researchers guess that over half the Congolese follow some form of Christianity, with probably twice as many Roman Catholics as Protestants. Not more than 10% of the population are Muslim; they live mainly in the northeast corner of the country among the Azande.

The Roman Catholic and Protestant churches control a large proportion of the hospitals, dispensaries, and schools in the country that were built by mission stations and are still run largely by dedicated mission workers. Church workers have set up agricultural, stockbreeding, and housing projects for the Congolese. It is said that almost every president in Africa is the product of a missionary education.

Butembo Mosque, one of many places of worship built for the Muslims in the country.

KIMBANGUIST CHURCH

The full title of Kimbanguism is The Sect of the Church of Jesus Christ on Earth through the Prophet Simon Kimbangu. This is the largest independent African church. It was founded by Simon Kimbangu who grew up in a Baptist Missionary Society mission. He became famous as a preacher and healer among the Kongo people. The thousands who came to hear his preaching called him *Ngunza*, the Kikongo word for prophet. Though his message was in no way political, the Belgian authorities became alarmed by the large crowds he attracted and the occasional disturbances caused, so Kimbangu and his closest followers were arrested in September 1921. He spent the rest of his life in prison in what is now Lubumbashi and died there in October 1951.

His youngest son, Joseph Diangienda, founded the Kimbanguist Church and gained official recognition for it. It was the first African church to be admitted (in 1969) to the World Council of Churches. The church has spread widely in Central Africa. Its creed rejects violence, polygamy, magic and witchcraft, alcohol, tobacco, and dancing. The worship is Baptist in form; communion was introduced in 1971. The Kimbanguist Church supports a large amount of social work in agriculture, healing, education, and youth work.

JAMAA

While most Catholic mission work was done in rural areas, the Jamaa ("ja-MAH") movement has recruited members largely from the mining complex area of Gécamines in Shaba province (formerly Katanga). A simple Franciscan missionary from Belgium, Father Placied Tempels, preached to a growing congregation that believed increasingly in his message of fraternity, a union of fellowship not unlike that of the early Church in Jerusalem. In 1954, seven married Catholic couples in Ruwe, near Kolwezi in South Katanga, formed the new movement. *Jamaa* is the Kiswahili word for family. The converts call each other *baba* and *mama*, Kiswahili for father and mother. The Virgin Mary is often referred to by her Bantu name, *mama Maria*. Their creed is embraced in the three themes of life, fecundity, and vital union. Faith must be lived and discovered through sharing in the Christian community, and from this relationship come children: not newborn babies but newborn adults, all part of an evergrowing, spiritual family. Since all members join as married couples, women assume a much higher status than is usual in Congolese society.

Father Tempels held that the strength of Jamaa came from the fellowship within African culture. Although he used the framework of the Catholic Church in which all are considered members of the same spiritual family, Tempels said the role of the priest was less centrally important than it usually is in Catholicism. He published his thinking in a book called *Bantu Philosophy,* but this met with considerable opposition, especially among the hierarchy of the local Catholic Church. How dared this simple Franciscan friar instruct his religious seniors on the merits of a so-called Bantu culture? Though the charismatic Jamaa movement has continued to grow, Tempels was forcibly retired to Belgium in 1962.

SUPERSTITION

Although African people would call it by many other names, superstition still plays a major part in their lives. If the Creator has little interest in puny human beings, as many believe, then it is up to humans to guard themselves against evil spirits. So amulets or fetishes are not considered magic; they are objects filled with power put there by the blessing of a diviner or holy man. The charm-seller in the market place is making available wise advice on how to avoid danger. Many believe in a special evil spirit, often called *li* ("LEE"), who lives in the stomach of certain people and gives them an urge to wander around and create mischief. If such people can obtain a lock of hair, a fingernail clipping, or a piece of clothing of a person, then they may cast a spell that can lead to sickness or death. For this reason all cuttings on the floor of a barber shop are burned.

A hand-colored woodcut of the 1800s shows a shaman invoking the spirits in the rain.

The Ngbandi tribal spirit is a snake, and the Ngbandi believe all twins are snakes. Therefore a twin dare not kill a snake for that would be akin to killing himself. The Mbuti Pygmies of the Ituri forest perform a special dance before they go hunting to apologize to the animal spirit they are going to kill. Travelers throw a stone in every stream they cross to thank the river god for keeping the water flowing. Many of the tribes along the Congo River believe in the mermaid-like Mamawata, who may bring wealth or death. Images of her are sold as good-luck charms. This fear may have its origin in the slave merchants who came like "white spirits" out of the waterways and stole young men.

A missionary worker takes stock of her supplies in a dispensary in Kamina, a town in Shaba province.

STATE VERSUS CHURCH

Once described in the Book of Common Prayer as "the Church Militant," missionary establishments in the Congo region have not been without controversy. For a while there was rivalry between Catholic and Protestant missionaries. There were claims that Protestants wanted to see the end of Belgian rule in the Congo, while the Catholic schools were careful to teach subservience and loyalty to *Bula Matari* (the state).

Without doubt, those in missionary work represented a large proportion of the educated adults in the country. At the time of independence in 1960 it was estimated that 15% of the non-African workforce was connected to the church. There were 7,500 missionaries in the Belgian Congo of which 6,000 were Catholic, many active in the health sector. In 1937 native Congolese priests numbered only 37; there were nearly 400 by 1960.

Church leaders in Africa have seldom hesitated to assume a role as guardians of the public conscience. One thinks of Archbishop Desmond

MOBUTU WORSHIP

The adulation (by order) of President Mobutu resulted in his being regarded almost as a god. The state-controlled media spoke of him as "the Guide, the Father of the Nation, the Chief, the Helmsman" and virtually as a Messiah. "God has sent a great prophet, our prestigious Guide Mobutu" was the belief officially encouraged. Press releases about the president used capital letters when referring to "Him." They encouraged the population to replace crucifixes with a picture of Mobutu. His mother, Mama Yemo, was compared to the Virgin Mary. Millions across the country wore shirts printed with his picture.

Tutu who denounced apartheid in South Africa for so many years. In the 1970s in Mobutu's Zaïre, Cardinal Malula did much to Africanize Christian church rituals and introduce a totally African leadership in the church—despite an ongoing feud with the president.

President Mobutu, a staunch Catholic, did all he could to reduce the power of the church. As part of his Africanization program, it was decreed that everyone born after February 16, 1972, should be given names commemorating their ancestors, not Christian saints. In 1972, all religious radio and television programs were banned, and religious youth groups were forbidden in favor of "youth party branches." "It is the MPR and not the Church that will lead the way," said Mobutu.

A count revealed Congolese religious affiliations in these proportions: Roman Catholic 50%, Protestant 20%, Kimbanguist 10%, Muslim 10%, other syncretic sects and traditional beliefs 10%.

The Lishala Cathedral School choir poses outside the cathedral. Many young Congolese receive a Christian missionary education.

87

LANGUAGE

AFRICA HAS OVER 1,700 distinct languages—this is almost a third of all the languages in the world. In the Democratic Republic of the Congo well over 200 languages and dialects are spoken. Nearly all belong to what linguistic scholars call the Niger-Congo subclassification, except for Kiswahili, which came through Arab influence in East Africa.

THE LANGUAGES IN USE

There is no national Congolese or Zaïrean language (as Spain has Spanish or Portugal has Portuguese). The most commonly used language is French, but it is somewhat despised as a colonial language forced on the country by European conquerors. It is the principal business and social language, but even today there are many Congolese who do not speak French.

Bantu languages use prefixes for shades of meaning in the way that most European languages use suffixes. So in the language of the Kongo, the people are Bakongo and the language Kikongo—"Ba" being a plural prefix and "Ki" indicating a language. Kikongo is spoken by about 2.5 million people.

Left and opposite: **Because educational facilities were introduced by missionaries, the lingua franca in the country became French. Many young Congolese are still educated by French missionaries.**

Some tribes used to communicate over quite long distances by using a "talking drum." This was a carved wooden drum with a split down the middle, leaving one side thicker than the other. When struck, each side produced a different tone, the thicker side more high-pitched. These two tones correspond with the basic tones of the language.

Hundreds of regional languages are used in addition to the local one. In Kinshasa and along the Congo River as far as Kisangani, Lingala ("lin-GAH-lah") is spoken. Kikongo is spoken in the southwest between Kinshasa and the Atlantic, a reminder of the Kongo kingdom that once existed there. In East and West Kasai in the southern center of the country, Tshiluba is the most common tongue. The influence of the slavers from the Zanzibar coast is clear in Kivu and the eastern border region, as well as around Lubumbashi, where Kiswahili is widely used as a first or second language. Around Goma people speak Nandé ("NAN-day").

It is thought that the Pygmy peoples once spoke a language related to the Khoisan of the so-called Bushmen in South Africa, though many centuries ago many of them adopted the Niger-Congo tongue of their neighbors. The localized Ngbandi tongue of the northern forest lands has grown into Sango, a widespread language in the Central African Republic and in Chad as well.

Nearly all Congolese languages and dialects derive from a Bantu base and are therefore "tonal" languages. This means that each word form can be pronounced in four or five different tones to give different shades of meaning. The pitch of the voice determines the exact meaning of a word or phrase. Therefore the language (and humor) is full of double meanings.

KISWAHILI

Kiswahili arrived in the Congo region as the language of the slave trading caravans from Zanzibar, where it had developed as a mixture of African and Arab vocabulary. The Arabic word *sawahili* means "of the coast" and there is a group of Swahili people on the east coast of Tanzania. Kiswahili is now far more than a tribal language. It is rapidly becoming one of the international languages of Africa, spoken by almost 50 million people, although not always as a mother tongue. However, its use is not yet widespread in the Democratic Republic of the Congo.

AFRICANIZATION

In an attempt to rid his country of colonial influence, Mobutu aimed to "Africanize" all names under the cry of *authenticité* ("OR-then-TISS-ee-tay," authenticity). So the capital city of Léopoldville became Kinshasa, Elisabethville became Lubumbashi, and Stanleyville was transformed into Kisangani. The province of Katanga was changed to Shaba, the Kiswahili word for copper.

After Mobutu met with Uganda's president, Lakes Albert and Edward were renamed Lake Mobutu Sese Seko and Lake Idi Amin Dada. All his people were ordered to replace their Christian names with African ones: so Joseph Désiré Mobutu became Mobutu Sese Seko. His full "praise name" was announced as Mobutu Sese Seko Koko Ngbendu wa za Banga. Mobutu adopted his soon famous leopard-skin cap as a visual indication of his African-ness, much as Jomo Kenyatta's fly-whisk did in Kenya. Today Kabila wants the Zaïre River to be called the Congo once again.

Multilingual advertising on the banner and street signs mounted against overhanging roof eaves.

Kinshasa has two daily papers: Salongo *in the mornings and* Elima *in the evenings.* Lubumbashi *has the daily* Njumbe *and Kisangani has* Boyoma.

ZAÏRE

Mobutu named the country and its great river Zaïre because he thought that Zaïre was more African. In fact, it is a Portuguese mispronunciation of the ancient Kikongo word *nzere* or *nzadi*, meaning "the river that swallows all rivers." The currency was also called the zaïre, and so were the local cigarettes and gasoline. Naming the money after the country's most vital geographic element has some interesting parallels: in South Africa the currency is the rand, the common name for the goldmining area of the Witwatersrand, while in Botswana the currency is pula, meaning "rain," something more precious than gold.

Four men in a doorway seem to be making a statement that blends in with the signs around them.

The country underwent many name changes: the Republic of the Belgian Congo became the Federal Republic of the Congo upon independence. After Mobutu seized power in 1965, it was the Democratic Republic of the Congo, then in 1971 the Republic of Zaïre. In 1997, President Kabila restored the name Democratic Republic of the Congo.

GREETINGS

"Peace be unto you" is followed by courteous inquiries about the family, and the other's health and prosperity. The answer is always that things are fine, "Thanks be to God." It would be exceedingly bad manners to talk business without a proper greeting.

The Congolese, like other Africans, insist on shaking hands. On entering a room, a man extends greetings and shakes the hand of all other men. To indicate warm friendship, the two may clap first before shaking hands. Men and women do not usually shake hands, unless the woman holds out her hand first, which is likely only if she is a close friend or very modern in outlook. A sign of respect to an elder is to hold out a fist to be shaken, indicating that you consider your hand too "dirty" to be worthy of contact. Those who have absorbed more of the French customs may greet with a kiss on the cheek, done two or three times, starting with the left cheek.

The commonest greeting is the Kiswahili *Jambo!* ("YAM-boh") or Hello! to which the reply is *Jambo-sana!* ("YAM-boh SAH-nah") or Hello very much! In Lingala, the greeting is *mbote* ("m-BOH-tay") and in Nandé, *wavuskiry* ("wah-voos-KEE-ray").

Two men stand in the doorway of a store selling men's clothes.

To maintain eye contact during a conversation is considered a sign of confrontation or bluff.

ARTS

TRADITIONAL ART consists mostly of items used for ceremonial occasions or else for more everyday activities such as singing, dancing, or storytelling. They often have a mix of magical and religious significance. Wood carvings are some of the most striking examples of African art.

Various themes are clear in the art of the Congo region, whether ancient or modern. One is the eternal struggle between the forces of order and control against the wild, uncontrolled chaos that threatens from outside. For example, the masks worn at the start of the initiation rites for Congolese boys are made of rough materials, while those worn at the end are of carved wood with more human faces, signifying initiation into civilized society. Masks served to protect the common people from the power of those who wore them—the king or the priest—and to echo the characters of the creatures who lived around them.

Left: **These artifacts demonstrate the artistic skills of the Congolese.**

Opposite: **A Buli Master's stool from the Luba-Henba people, a museum treasure today.**

A tribal dancer with an oval mask is fully clad in regalia for a festival.

TRIBAL SPECIALITIES

Individual art styles are influenced by the materials available, by lifestyle, and the culture of the artist.

In the rainforests of the northern region, the Komo people create wooden masks, weapons, and fetishes. A style emerged here, possibly brought by migrants from Nigeria, of a heart-shaped face, with the two eye sockets at the top and the mask narrowing to a chin and mouth at the base. Much of the Komo craftwork is associated with the rituals of their soothsayers or healers who are adorned with feathers, bark belts, and ivory bracelets, and little bells hanging from armbands. On the edge of the forest, the Mangbetu, of Sudanese origin, wear hardly any clothing in their ritual dances but instead paint the whole body in elaborate geometric patterns and braid their hair into a tall wicker-work frame stuck with ivory or wooden pins.

The lower reaches of the Congo River were influenced by the Portuguese who introduced Christianity. Some Christian visual signs were adopted and given an African symbolism. In Kongo woodcarving, admired for its realism and relatively more relaxed poses of the human figures, the cross or crucifix is a symbol of power.

From the Pende people, east of Kinshasa, come wooden masks with distinctive, heavy-lidded eyes and grotesque features—features admired and copied by Picasso in the years after 1906. The Pende also weave fawn and black striped coverings for the whole body from raffia, leaves, and feathers; these are used by dancers in circumcision rituals. Since the Pende carvers are considered to have special powers and are thus respected in their village, onlookers are fearful of the dancers as well, as if they too have taken on some unknown spirit power.

The savanna region of Kasai is home to such old tribes as the Luba and Kuba. Luba masks were the first Central African art to be recognized internationally. Their now well-known, hemispherical masks have protruding eyes and exaggerated nose and mouth features, sometimes painted black with white parallel lines. Few of those on sale in the street markets are Luba carvings: they are backstreet copies made anywhere in West or Central Africa. Anything original and genuinely old is safe in a museum, such as the Académie des Beaux-Arts in Kinshasa.

Kuba, like Kongo, was once a powerful kingdom. Much of its craftwork was developed to please or adorn royalty, and carving became a much respected art form. One carver in each reign was given the honor of carving a statue of the king who dressed in sumptuous costumes and wore royal masks shaped like helmets with the face covered by leopard skin, decorated with beads and cowries, and crowned with a crest of eagle feathers. Even today, some traditional masks may only be worn by those of the royal line. The Kuba style is highly decorative with many geometric patterns. Kuba artisans create a variety of objects: wooden cups, ornate boxes, game boards, drums, pipes, stools, and fancy spoons.

Chokwe tribesmen with painted bodies practice their drumming.

MUSIC OF AFRICA

Music and dance go together in the Congo. Nobody can listen to music without hand-clapping, foot-stamping, singing, or dancing to the rhythm. Usually there will be a drum of some shape, probably played by hand, and an assortment of other percussion instruments such as rattles, bells, a wooden xylophone, and resonant blocks. In ritual dances there is sometimes a particular drumbeat associated with the ancestral spirit or power involved. The drummer must know each special rhythm.

Traditional dance is usually part of a social ritual or festive celebration. For example, the Salampasu people of the Kasai district are proud that they were once fierce warriors renowned for beheading their enemies. The men, dressed in fiber costumes adorned with leopard skins, perform wild masked dances in which they brandish fearsome-looking swords to maintain their reputation. The Kuba dancers perform in order to give regal status to the royal masks, so their dance is a sequence of complex routines presented with great dignity. Part of their costume is a huge feather crest

MUSIC WITH A BEAT

The pounding beat of much of our modern pop music has its origin in Africa, and Kinshasa is the music capital of Africa. There is a Latin-American influence too, which results in a similarity to rumba music. This style was introduced when radio stations played music by the early Cuban rumba bands. Local groups imitated the rhythm, often playing in what became called Congo bars. A solo guitar might be accompanied by some lively brass instruments. The beat was provided by drums or rattles or even bottles struck to produce a particular note.

With the arrival of the acoustic guitar and electric amplifiers, the bands became larger and more successful. The ability to improvize with whatever instruments are available, combined with an appreciation of the complex African rhythms, has created what is today called Afro-Pop.

with red interwoven ribbons. Near the eastern Great Rift Valley lakes, it is the initiation dances that predominate. Boys and girls aged 10 to 12 paint white spots on their bodies and perform dances with elaborate waist girdles of cloth and beads, all as part of their initiation from childhood to maturity.

The *kalimba* ("ka-LIM-bah"), or lamellaphone, a sort of thumb-piano with hand-plucked metal strips set against a wooden soundboard, is heard everywhere. The Congolese also love local, home-created village music from flutes made of wood, bamboo, or reed. Panpipes, horns, and single-stringed resonators are popular too.

Congo music stays at the top of the pop charts in Africa. Some modern Congo music uses no musical instruments, like that of Zap Mama, an all-female group whose music is based on traditional Pygmy music.

Above: **A wall mosaic depicting women's agricultural activities decorates a public building in Kinshasa.**

Opposite: **A Mount Hoyo Pygmy sells tribal masks and other carvings to tourists.**

PAINTING

Paint is expensive, so it needs to have a practical use. Advertising is an obvious one. Since artists' colors and canvas are expensive, Congolese artists paint on the walls of houses using ordinary commercial paint, bright colors, and mostly the flat, childlike style of folk art. They choose themes that will attract customers. For hairdressers, they paint the range of ladies' hairstyles. A café may have pictures of favorite musicians or sports stars.

Many artists struggling to make a living in Kinshasa prefer to paint scenes with some sort of social significance. They see themselves as commentators or critics of the world around them.

Cheri Samba, an internationally known Congolese artist, paints portraits, usually from photographs, and wall signs. He likes to include some social or political message on issues such as drug addiction, abuse of power, bribery, or AIDS. He claims to take his inspiration from reality and enjoys including the comic side of life.

Kasongo (many Congolese prefer to be known by one name only) concentrates on paintings of the violence and cruelty that erupted when Belgian paratroopers took the city of Lubumbashi in 1964. He shows the brutal beatings of civilians fleeing from a pipe-smoking figure representing Henry Stanley, the symbol of colonization.

The venerable Kalume is gentler-minded. He creates wall-paintings of rivers and landscapes, often with a religious significance.

In a lighter mood, Sim Simaro likes to paint buses. Since he enjoys traveling himself, he details all sorts of transportation problems, providing scenes of life in Kinshasa today.

CARVING

Wood is the most easily available material in the Congo region, so most of the craftwork offered to tourists or exhibited in the country's few museums are highly polished wood carvings. Masks, known generally as *mbuya*, are by far the most common. Some masks bear the scarification marks peculiar to a tribe, such as the body patterns of the Bena Lulua or the Mangbetu of the northeast. The masks made by the Bapuma people copy the cuts they make on the forehead between the eyes and on the temples. These masks usually have a cloth attached that completely encloses the dancer, who often performs on stilts.

Beads are used to create objects such as necklaces, bangles, and headdresses, which by their patterns and colors represent spiritual values vital to the community. Such items play major roles in community rituals such as birth, circumcision, marriage, and death. Other craft items include boxes, carved doors, necklaces made of glass beads, copper or shells, as well as dark green Malachite jewelry from the southern Shaba region. There is very little carved from ivory, and most metalwork tends to be for daily use rather than anything decorative.

LEISURE

THE CONCEPT of organized leisure activities would seem strange to most Congolese. For the many who are unemployed, the entire day is leisure. For those who work daily to grow food at subsistence level, there is no leisure time. The weekly break from work for many is attendance at church, when everyone wears his or her best clothes.

CHILDREN AT PLAY

Congolese youngsters play mostly in imitation of adults. Girls practice carrying loads on their head and play "making families." Boys make their own bows and arrows to practice hunting and are wildly excited if they return home with a kill. They climb trees and run races. And always, everywhere, the boys play soccer. The ball may be a bundle of rags tied with coarse string or a cheap plastic ball from the market, but soccer stars are their heroes. From this they grow up with a sense of fair play.

Left: **Young boys in school uniform practice table tennis without a table on the street.**

Opposite: **A young boy proudly holds up his home-made toy truck, which will keep him entertained for hours.**

To young Congolese men motorcycles are not only a convenient mode of transportation. As in other urban centers, the motorcycle is often associated with "macho" men.

MANKALA

King Shamba Bulongongo of the Bakuba was said to have diverted his people's attention from gambling by introducing the mankala ("man-KAH-la") board. Mankala is a game similar to backgammon and is played with regional variations all over Africa. It is supposed to have originated in Egypt thousands of years ago. Usually two people play, although teams can play taking turns. Above all, it requires time.

The board consists of two rows of six cups, or more simply, holes are made in the ground. To start, four beans—or pebbles or marbles or dried peas—are placed in each cup. The first player takes all the beans from any cup on his side of the board and drops them one at a time in each neighboring cup to the right, that is, moving counterclockwise. He makes a capture when the last bean dropped falls in a cup on his opponent's side that contains only one or two beans.

The basic idea is to strategize in such a way as to make this happen, but there are regional variations and only a mankala player can explain them fully. The result is a game as complex and absorbing as chess. Village players may be unable to read or write but they can out-think any visitor at mankala!

SPORTS

If the national game is mankala, the national sport is soccer. The Democratic Republic of the Congo is as soccer-crazy as any country in Africa. President Mobutu was fiercely proud of the Leopards, the national soccer team. While the rebel forces were fighting their way across the country, the national soccer team still played its qualifying matches in the World Cup, and the players in their yellow shirts and red shorts were national heroes far more popular than any politician. It was inevitable that the war situation eventually affected financial support for the national team. In August 1997, FIFA (the world governing body for soccer) ranked the Democratic Republic of the Congo 77 in the world rankings, 18 among African countries. In Africa, Morocco ranked first and Zambia second.

In Kinshasa there is an impressive stadium that Mobutu built to host the 1974 world heavyweight championship fight between Muhammed Ali and George Foreman—remembered in boxing history as the "Rumble in the Jungle." He considered both fighters to be "sons of Africa" and was proud that the first such championship in Africa should be in Zaïre.

Table soccer provides youngsters with a popular form of entertainment.

A TRADITIONAL MAKERE FOLKTALE

A mother once had two sons. The younger one went to visit his uncle's compound where his uncle served him a feast of chicken and millipedes (a special delicacy), after which he told the young man to sleep in the chicken run. Next morning the uncle told him to select an egg. The young man chose a small one. His uncle was pleased and told him to throw the egg on the ground on the way home in the place where the ruins of an old settlement stood. So the young man did so and at once neat new houses rose out of the earth. From each came a beautiful woman, slaves bowed to him as their master, and the young man became a great chief.

In due course, the elder brother visited his younger brother and asked how he obtained his wealth. The young man told him the story and pointed out the way to their uncle's place. The uncle embraced his elder nephew and offered him chicken and millipedes. The elder brother ate the chicken but refused the millipedes. He also refused to sleep in the chicken run and demanded a proper bed. When offered an egg the next morning, he chose the biggest he could find. When he went into the bush and broke the egg, armed men came out who grew into giants in a few moments and killed him.

Learn, therefore, that good manners and modesty pay off!

This brief story has the typical folktale framework of a good man and a bad one with a journey or quest that imparts knowledge. The benefits of good manners and undemanding behavior as a guest are clearly indicated. Note the acceptance of slavery as a desirable part of wealth, as well as having plenty of wives!

STORYTELLING

Storytelling remains popular in the Democratic Republic of the Congo. The traditional folklore story conveys some piece of wisdom or social advice through a simple, often magical, tale. The storyteller is usually elderly and respected, with the skill to create different characters with his voice and the noises of jungle animals as well if required. One favorite tale is the story of the Creator god who had four children: Raffia-palm, Liana, Wine-palm, and Oil-palm, his favorite.

In modern times a new kind of storytelling has emerged. Instead of traditional folklore around the fire at night, there is a call for modern stories for adults. In a bar or café, someone known as a good storyteller will be persuaded to tell a story of recent troubled history or a legend of unrespected politicians. Such a story may be interrupted as the teller refuses to finish unless more tobacco or beer is provided.

NIGHT LIFE

The Congolese love dancing and they do it in a frenzied fashion. What the Kinshasans call *kwasa kwasa* music is the favorite. Bars that offer dancing as well as drinking are known as *ngandas* ("un-GAN-dahs"). Nightclubs have theatrical lighting and floor shows, charge astronomical prices, and provide military-style doormen. Though the classier establishments stay open until midnight, most customers leave by 9 p.m. for fear of late-night robbers.

In the old Cité district, there are open-air roadside gigs, rooftop terraces, underground dives, and dance places. *La Maison Blanche* has the largest auditorium so visiting groups often choose to perform there.

A young woman entertainer performs in a jazzy nightclub.

FESTIVALS

MANY CONGOLESE may wonder at the meaning of festivals as there seems precious little to celebrate. There are no grand cultural events and no street parades apart from marching troops.

OFFICIAL OCCASIONS

The calendar provides an impressive list of official public holidays. These fall into two clear categories: Christian festivals or celebrations of the Mobutu regime and Mobutu himself. It is unclear what the new Kabila regime will want to celebrate. For instance, MPR Day honors the one-party state. The *Mouvement Populaire de la Révolution* was the sole political party for most of Mobutu's time and Kabila has indicated that he will eventually allow multiparty politics.

Opposite: **A combination of the traditional and the modern, this woman celebrant in a street festival dons a mask that resembles the tribal masks used in villages.**

PUBLIC HOLIDAYS IN ZAÏRE

- January 1
  New Year's Day

- January 4
  Day of the Martyrs for
  Independence

- May 1
  Labor Day

- May 20
  MPR Day

- June 24
  Zaïre Day

- June 30
  Independence Day

- August 1
  Parents' Day

- October 14
  President's Birthday

- November 17
  Armed Forces Day

- November 24
  Anniversary of the New Regime

RELIGIOUS HOLIDAYS
Easter Monday
Ascension Day
Whit Monday
Christmas Day

INDEPENDENCE DAY

Independence Day remembers the 1960 break from colonialism, while Zaïre Day has become Democratic Republic of the Congo Day, a celebration of the nation itself. Mobutu used these days for military parades and a show of power. The flag would be ceremoniously raised and the national anthem sung. The anthem during Mobutu's time was *"Zaïrois, dans la paix retrouvée, peuple uni, nous sommes zaïrois"* (Zaïreans, in peace found again, a united people, we are Zaïreans); the words and tune were composed by Bolla Di Mpasi Londi.

Congolese national holidays and parades are accompanied by flag waving. The country has had four different flags in the last 100 years. The first flag of the independent Congo was light blue with a gold five-pointed star in the center and six smaller stars down the left edge. In 1971, Mobutu created a green flag with a yellow circle in the middle showing a dark brown hand waving the flaming red torch of freedom. Kabila's alliance reintroduced the flag of independent Congo, except that it is dark blue.

RELIGIOUS DAYS

The Roman Catholic Church is careful to observe its main feast days of Christmas (the birth of Jesus), Lent (his temptations in the wilderness), Good Friday and Easter (his death and resurrection), and Whitsunday (his ascension into heaven). The actual calendar days of these celebrations vary from year to year. Depending on the resources available, there may be special services of Mass with communion and processions.

The same religious festivals are observed by the Protestant churches, though usually with less ceremony.

Christmas and New Year's Day are celebrated in all African countries, but Mobutu, as part of his Africanization program, tried to change the Christmas celebrations to Zaïre Day on June 24, the birthday of the country's constitution. This was resisted.

For Congolese Christian families religious holidays are special days; they wear their best clothes to church and gather to sing songs in a communal celebration.

CHRISTMAS IN A ZAÏREAN VILLAGE

Although there is no guarantee that the same festivities still occur, until recently there were still some Congolese villages that put on a dramatized version of the Christmas story and celebrate with caroling.

When it is time for the play to begin, a drum beats out an invitation. The whole village may take part in the action: all are counted by the tax-collectors and follow the actors to each new scene. The actors playing Joseph and Mary are told there is no room in any house for them, so they go to a specially built shelter made of palm branches and decorated with flowers. Here there is a cradle holding a real baby.

While the watching villagers sing, shepherds appear with live goats and bow to the family. Then come the Wise Men wearing twisted scarfs of bright colors, carrying black native pots and gourds as their gifts.

FAMILY FESTIVALS

The most common events of a "festival" nature take place around family celebrations such as weddings, baptisms, and funerals. For the Congolese, there are speeches, drinking, appropriate singing, and usually dancing as well (except at funerals). Guests at a baptism are expected to bring a gift for both the proud parents; money is quite acceptable. After the church service, there is a celebratory meal.

The proper celebrations required after a wedding are so expensive that many men cannot afford to get married until later in life. Before the wedding itself, there would be up to a week of parties, visits to relatives, and the exchange of gifts of money or livestock. After the ceremony, held in a church or at the mayor's office, close friends and relations go to a suitable house for the final round of eating and dancing. Presents from the groom to the bride's family may cost the equivalent of several hundred US dollars—an astronomical sum for a man whose annual income may be only US$200 or less.

Funerals are more solemn events. The Congolese believe in burying their dead. There is no thought of cremation. This is a sacred duty to the deceased who is now one of the revered ancestors. Even a riverboat, which is run commercially, will anchor briefly to allow a dead passenger to be properly buried on shore.

Local communities also host fairs called fêtes. These celebrate an event such as the end of the harvest season. Hopefully, it is the season of plenty, so it is a suitable time to celebrate. There are traditional dances, in the local style, together with plenty of a sour, thick beer and a feeling of relaxation that the harvest is over. Libations may be poured on the earth and ancestors thanked by name.

The toast, whatever the language, will mean, "Drink with me. I am alive and so are you. Let us enjoy life together."

ITUL

The Itul is a rare dance festival of the Kuba people that is held only when the king gives permission. This infrequent occurrence is probably because of the extensive preparation and cost involved. It is usually danced only by the children of the royal family and may be a private occasion inside the palace with the king's wives taking part as dancers and singers. Or it may be held in a courtyard open to the public. During the months of rehearsal, those involved are paid and special costumes are designed and made.

A symbolic animal is chosen as the "enemy-animal," and the center of the dance area represents the lair of this animal. The performance has two parts, presented on consecutive days. On the first day, there are lamentations on the destruction caused by this animal. The dancers wear red, the color of mourning. Their intricate singing and dancing patterns are accompanied by rhythmic drumming—on special drums that can only be used by the sons or grandsons of kings. On the second day, the dresses have changed to skirts of raffia embroidered in black with geometric lines and symbols. The animal is confronted and hunted. It seizes one of the dancers. With a flurry of shrieks and gunshots it is finally killed and its body is presented to the king.

The Itul festival has little religious significance, but impresses more by the rarity of the performance, its exclusive quality, traditional formality, and the glorification of the royal family.

FOOD

THE VAST MAJORITY of the Congolese are underfed and suffering from poor health as a result of an insufficiently nutritious diet. If half a mother's children survive beyond the age of 5, she considers herself fortunate. The idea of providing children with a balanced diet is both unknown and impossible.

The Congolese eat what they can gather or grow. Too many children, especially those in the refugee camps, suffer from the protein deficiency usually known by its Ghanaian name *kwashiorkor* ("KWAHSH-ee-or-kor"), which stunts body growth and causes the muscles to waste away.

The Congolese will cook and eat tree-living grubs, monitor lizards, bats, and rats. Almost anything will go into the stew pot that simmers on an open fire or a wood-burning stove. To a Westerner, such a diet might seem to indicate a desperation to eat anything; the Congolese, on the other hand, appreciates the bountiful diversity of food from nature.

Left: **A village boy displays a bat he has just caught. The Congolese can find culinary uses for many native creatures.**

Opposite: **An assortment of vibrant colors—the women's colorful clothes and the nuts and beans catch the eye in Kamina market.**

FOOD GATHERING

In the Democratic Republic of the Congo people such as the Pygmies do not practice the skills of modern agriculture, while others plant only enough for their needs and keep cattle in an unsystematic way. Their aim is to produce "enough." In many places it is not possible to produce a surplus for sale or a better quality for increased health and nutrition. Representatives of foreign aid organizations have tried to upgrade the farming techniques but have found this difficult.

EVERYDAY FARE

The main meal, eaten in the evening, consists of a filling staple food such as rice or cassava, with a bowl of sauce for extra taste, and perhaps some vegetables, fish, or meat. These protein foods flavor the meal; they are not the main items as in a Western diet. In many parts of the Democratic Republic of the Congo more fish is eaten than meat. Of the staple foods, rice is the most common and the most popular, but it is also the most expensive because nearly all rice is imported.

Cassava is common and cheap; when cooked it makes a sticky white mound a bit like bread dough. Bananas are sometimes mixed with mashed plantains or cassava. Young green okra pods (also called gumbo) are used as a staple vegetable, even if they are a bit slimy when cooked. The Congolese enjoy their food spicy-hot; they also have a peanut-based sauce that is usually milder.

A villager heads home with a harvest of cassava.

The meats available include almost anything from woodland or forest, as well as chickens, the occasional duck or goose, and the rare treat of beef. The Congolese are particularly fond of eating monkey, but will happily feast on porcupine, crocodile, or antelope. Pigeons, rats, locusts, and mopane worms are on the menu when available. If they kill an elephant or a chimpanzee for food, which they do for the flesh is tasty, the meat is smoke-cured to disguise it; these animals are listed as endangered species and the hunter might be fined.

Fruit is eaten often, although the idea of a dessert course is not usual. Bananas are popular, cooked or raw. Virtually all other tropical fruit are available: pineapples, papayas, avocado, oranges, as well as coconuts.

To the Congolese, ants are a delicacy, raw or roasted. The man in the picture holds a tin full of ants for his meal while he adeptly grasps a locust between his fingers—another treat.

CASSAVA

The most common staple food in the country is cassava (also called manioc), which is filling but has limited nutritional value. Many malnourished children owe their lack of growth to a diet of cassava and little else. The Congolese make a flour from its tuberous roots and cook it into a starchy gruel. Dried, ground cassava makes a sort of flour known as *farine de manioc* ("fah-REEN duh MAN-ee-oh") that can be stored. Before cooking, it needs to be soaked in salted water when it swells to about double its size. The Congolese also soak cassava leaves in boiling water to remove the acetic acid, then pound them to a pulp and cook them with palm oil to produce a green vegetable that resembles spinach. Fermented cassava is used to make an alcoholic drink. In Western countries, cassava powder is better known as tapioca.

Villagers wash and slice fish by the village stream. Fish is a common item in the Congolese diet.

WELCOME TO OUR HUMBLE HOME

A typical meal in a rural household—usually the only meal of the day in many homes—is served from a bowl on the ground. Those eating the meal wash their hands first and usually take off their shoes before sitting on the mats. They eat with the right hand, often tucking the left hand behind the back. Each person takes a small handful of the rice or cassava, dips it into the sauce or meat, forms it into a ball, and then eats it. Visitors will be served first by the head of the household. After the meal, a washbasin will be passed around.

Breakfast and lunch may be dry cakes of cassava or some fruit. The cooked meal comes in the early evening. Freshwater fish is eaten by many; a favorite is grilled perch or *capitaine* ("KAP-ee-TAYN"). A family living close to the river will salt and dry any spare fish to preserve them, since few homes have electricity and even fewer have refrigerators. Long-brewed herbal tea is a cheap and refreshing drink. The Congolese use various leaves such as lemon grass to flavor the tea.

EATING OUT

Once, in Kinshasa, there were Italian, Greek, Chinese, French, and Portuguese restaurants. Even more popular were those offering African dishes such as cassava leaf stew or *saka saka* and wild game or *gibier* ("JEE-bee-ay"), all served with rice. Menus could include wild pig (like tough pork), impala (like tasty venison), or snake (salty and bony). When it is available, the favorite poultry is guinea fowl, which has a darker, stronger-tasting flesh than chicken. There might be roast fish flavored with hot chili and served with cassava porridge. A candidate for the national dish could be *moambé* ("MWAM-bay"), rice with a spicy sauce of peanuts and palm oil served usually with chicken or sometimes fish. Kinshasa residents enjoy cream-filled cakes and pastries, as well as ice cream. Bitter cola nuts, used as an appetite suppressant, and fresh fruit such as pineapple are always available.

The more usual method of eating out is to buy from the street-corner cooks who sell fried sweet potatoes or grilled skewers of unidentifiable meat or pidi-pidi ("PEE-dee PEE-dee"), sausages made of crushed peanuts and cassava, fried in palm oil and covered with spices. In the eastern towns, vendors cook bananas in melted butter and roll them in chopped peanuts.

A market vendor in a Kamina market displays a dried catfish.

DRINKS

Congolese like drinking beer, and customers are found in the numerous beer halls by 8 a.m. The other popular drink is palm wine. The juice is tapped from palm trees, mixed with yeast, allowed to ferment overnight, and then sold in jugs by the roadside. This is the cheap stuff, which is a bit fizzy and not unlike coconut milk. Mature palm wine has more of a taste of alcohol. Drunk cold, it is refreshing.

The Congolese have adopted the African ritual of swilling the last mouthful around in the bottom of the cup or glass and throwing it on the ground as a libation to the earth god, a sign of thanks.

Tap water is unsafe to drink.

Vegetable vendors hold packed boxes, resembling egg cartons, for sale in the market.

MOAMBÉ CHICKEN

one chicken
$1/2$ cup oil (the Congolese use palm oil, but vegetable
    cooking oil will do)
2 medium-sized onions, halved, with outer skin removed
2 cloves garlic, crushed
half a green pepper, fleshy pips removed, cut into pieces
2 chilies, crushed or 1 teaspoon cayenne pepper
    (reduce this if you do not like your sauce hot)
2 or 3 celery leaves
$1/2$ teaspoon ground nutmeg
1 small tin of tomato purée
3–4 cups chicken stock (you can add two bouillon cubes
    to water, or use the stock from boiling chicken)
$1^1/2$ cups peanut butter
salt and pepper

Start by cooking the chicken. Cook it whole, if possible, in a large pot with water, salt, and pepper. Bring it to the boil and remove any scum from the top of the liquid. Reduce the heat and allow it to simmer until the chicken is tender. This will take about an hour, depending on the size of the chicken.

While the chicken is simmering, start on the moambé sauce.

Heat the oil in a large frying pan and fry onions, garlic, pepper, chilies, and celery leaves until onions start to brown.

Next, add the ground nutmeg and tomato purée and cook for another two minutes, stirring occasionally.

Put the chicken stock into a saucepan, add the mixture from the pan and peanut butter, season with a shake of salt and pepper, and bring to a boil, stirring all the time. Remove from heat.

Drain the cooked chicken, then add it to the sauce and cook gently for about five more minutes.

Serve with rice. This dish can feed four to six people.

The oil palm is a favorite tree of the Congolese. They say "it strokes the stomach." Besides being a most valuable cash crop, no cooking is complete without palm oil. Palm oil is also used as a traditional medicine against scabies, and for making margarine and soap.

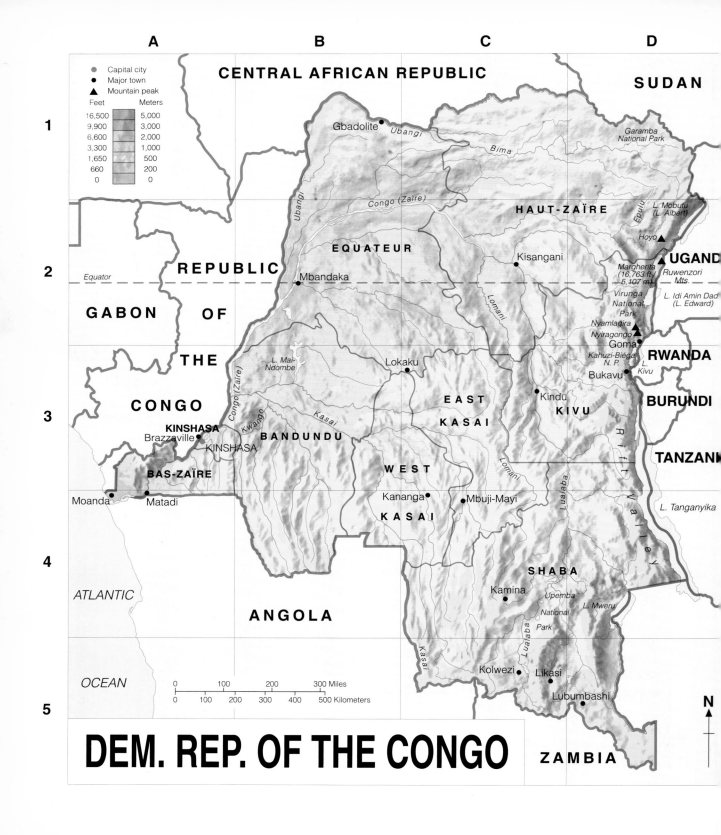

DEM. REP. OF THE CONGO

QUICK NOTES

OFFICIAL NAMES
Democratic Republic of the Congo/Republique
    Democratique du Congo (since 1997)
Republic of Zaïre (1971–97)
Democratic Republic of the Congo (1965–71)
Federal Republic of the Congo (1960–65)
Republic of the Belgian Congo (1908–60)
Congo Free State (1885–1908)

LAND AREA
905,567 square miles (2.35 million square km)

CAPITAL
Kinshasa

IMPORTANT CITIES
Lubumbashi, Kisangani, Mbuji-Mayi

PROVINCES
Bas-Zaïre, Bandundu, Equateur, Haut-Zaïre,
Kinshasa, Kivu, Shaba, East Kasai, West Kasai

MAJOR RIVERS
Congo (Zaïre), Ubangi, Kasai

MAJOR LAKES
Tanganyika, Idi Amin Dada (Edward), Mweru

HIGHEST POINT
Margherita Peak: 16,763 ft (5,107 m)

MAIN EXPORTS
Copper, coffee, diamonds, cobalt, crude oil

CURRENCY
New Zaïre = 100 makuta
1 US$ is approximately 113,000 NZ

NATIONAL FLAG
Dark blue with a gold five-pointed star in the
center and six small stars down the hoist edge.

NATIONAL ANTHEM (MOBUTU ERA)
*"Zaïrois, dans la paix retrouvée, peuple uni,
nous sommes zaïrois"* ("Zaïreans, in peace
found again, a united people, we are Zaïreans");
composed by Bolla Di Mpasi Londi

POPULATION
47 million (1997 estimate)

LIFE EXPECTANCY
47 years

MAJOR LANGUAGES
French, Lingala, Kingwana, Kikongo, Tshiluba

MAJOR RELIGIONS
Roman Catholic (50%), Protestant (20%),
Kimbanguist (10%), Islam (10%), other syncretic
sects and traditional beliefs (10%)

LITERACY RATE
Women, 68%; men, 87%

IMPORTANT POLITICAL LEADERS
Patrice Lumumba (1925–61): first prime minister
    after independence, June to September 1960
Joseph Kasavubu (1910?–69): first president
    after independence 1960–65
Moise Tshombe (1919–69): premier 1964–65
Mobutu Sese Seko (1930–97): president 1965–
    97
Laurent Kabila, president (1997–)

GLOSSARY

authenticité ("OR-then-TISS-ee-tay")
French word meaning authenticity, a movement initiated by Mobutu in the early 1970s to Africanize all names in the country.

capitaine ("KAP-ee-TAYN")
Grilled perch, a dish enjoyed by the Congolese.

cassava ("kass-AH-vah")
Root used as a staple food, also called manioc.

gibier ("JEE-bee-ay")
Wild game dish, usually served with rice.

gumbo
Young okra pods used as a staple vegetable; turns slimy when cooked.

jambo ("Yam-boh")
"Hello" in Kiswahili.

kalimba ("ka-LIM-bah")
Thumb-piano with hand-plucked metal strips set against a wooden soundboard.

Kikongo ("ki-KON-go")
A Congolese language spoken between Kinshasa and the coast, originating with the Kongo kingdom.

Kiswahili ("ki-swah-HEE-lee")
Widely used language in the eastern border region and in Lubumbashi in the southeast.

kleptocracy ("klep-TOK-ruh-see")
Government system that includes bribery and corruption.

kwasa kwasa
A kind of music enjoyed by the Kinshasans.

kwashiorkor ("KWAHSH-ee-or-kor")
A protein-deficiency disease that stunts body growth and causes the muscles to waste away.

li ("LEE")
Evil spirit believed to reside in the stomach of certain people.

mbote ("m-BOH-tay")
"Hello" in Lingala.

moambé ("MWAM-bay")
National dish: rice with a spicy sauce of peanuts and palm oil, served with chicken or fish.

Nandé ("NAN-day")
Language used around Goma, by Lake Kivu.

nganda ("un-GAN-dah")
Congolese bar offering dancing and drinking.

pillage ("pee-YAHJ")
French word meaning looting of shops and houses, especially during a time of chaos and disorder.

Tshiluba ("chi-LOO-bah")
A language of East and West Kasai.

Zaïre ("ZEYE-EER")
Former name of the Democratic Republic of the Congo; the currency; another name for Congo River.

BIBLIOGRAPHY

Grant, Neil. *Just Look At Life in the Rainforest.* Vero Beach, USA: Rourke Enterprises, 1987.

Jenike, David and Mark Jenike. *A Walk Through a Rain Forest: Life in the Ituri Forest in Zaire (A Cincinnati Zoo Book).* London: Franklin Watts, 1995.

Meditz, Sandra W. and Tim Merrill. Zaire: *A Country Study (Area Handbook Series).* Baton Rouge, Louisiana: Claitors Publishing Division, 1995.

Newton, Alex. *Central Africa.* Hawthorn, Australia: Lonely Planet, 1994.

Robbins, David. *Aspects of Africa.* London, England: Penguin, 1995.

Visual Geography Series. Zaire in Pictures. Minneapolis: Lerner Publications, 1993.

INDEX

INDEX

INDEX